THE TRUTH ABOUT:

ACCESSING NEW COVENANT WEALTH

Dr William C. Small

FirstWorld Publishing

Dallas, TX

The Truth About: Accessing New Covenant Wealth

Copyright © 2019 Dr William C. Small

ISBN – 13: 978-0-9972067-3-9

ISBN – 10: 0-9972067-3-X

Cover Photo: ©Istockphoto.com

Interior & cover design: First World Publishing

Unless otherwise indicated, all scripture quotations are from the King James Version of the Bible.

Scriptures were taken from the Thompson Chain-Reference Bible, Fifth Improved Edition, copyright © 1908, 1917, 1929, 1934, 1957, 1964, 1982, by Frank Charles Thompson.

CONTENTS

DEDICATION

To my daughter **Deandra** and her generation

QUOTES

"Wisdom is the principle thing, therefore get wisdom but in all of your getting get understanding." ~ **Proverbs 4:7**

"If you don't learn to handle finances you will never be a leader."
~ **Bishop T.D. Jakes**

"Money is usually attracted, not pursued." ~ **Jim Rohn**

"People's ideas on how to become a millionaire is designed to make them a millionaire not you." ~ **Dr Will**

"The night is far spent, the day is at hand: let us therefore cast off the works of darkness, and let us put on the armor of light." ~ **Romans 13:12**

"The fault, dear Brutus, is not in our stars, but in ourselves, that we are underlings." ~ **Cassius**

"People that have reached the pinnacle of their profession are the only ones who qualify to be a has been." ~ **Dr Will**

"What we really want to do is what we are really meant to do. When we do what we are meant to do, money comes to us, doors open for us, we feel useful, and the work we do feels like play to us." ~ **Julia Cameron**

"Change does not always lead to improvement but without change there can be no improvement." ~ **Dr Myles Munroe**

"The most powerful relationship you will ever have is the relationship with yourself." ~ **Steve Maraboli**

"Men are the foundation on which family wealth is built and women are the building on the foundation that retains and maintains wealth for the family. There can be cracks in the building but cracks in the foundation will cause the building to be condemned." ~ **Dr Will**

"He that has pity upon the poor lends unto the Lord; and that which he has given will HE [GOD] pay him again." ~ **Proverbs 19:17**

"Apple's core value is the belief that people with passion **can** change the world for the better." ~ **Steve Jobs**

INTRODUCTION

"But you shall remember the Lord your GOD: for it is HE that gives you power to get wealth that HE may establish HIS covenant (Deuteronomy 8:18)."

Before we begin let me share a little about myself so you will understand the value of what I am offering. I worked in the financial services industry for 15 years where I made over $100 million for my clients. I set myself up receive $81,000 a year in passive income. I don't have to do anything to get that money except wake up every morning. That does not include the money I make while sleeping from my books and CDs. If you put $81,000 in the context of a working man's annual income earned through working 8 hours day or 40 hours a week, I make $40 an hour. The average person who works at Ford or GM makes around $28 per hour. I receive $40 an hour while relaxing by my pool or cruising in my Jag because I had the foresight to obtain financial literacy early and work that knowledge diligently to make it profit me.

Women can benefit from this knowledge but whatever I produce is for men who want to be better men, husbands, fathers, and providers. Therefore, I must let men know right up front that it took me 45 years to get where I am. I understand that a young man today, especially the not so young man, does not have 45 years to learn what

4

they need to know to achieve financial freedom. So, I have written books and produced CDs to give men the ability to learn everything I know within a few hours of reading or listening. Again, to be totally up front and open I must tell you that it will take 3-5 years of diligently applying this information in order to master it to the point where you can also earn money while sleeping. So this is NOT a get rich QUICK scheme. You can earn money right away by applying the knowledge but it won't be much until you master it to the point of understanding. Once you understand it you will begin to generate high profits. So, I will be sharing information designed to in-form or generate internal growth and change. You will be conducting impartation through diligent application of the information to cause an acceleration of internal growth and change.

"Wisdom is the principle thing therefore get wisdom but in all of your getting get understanding (Proverbs 4:7)."

"If you don't learn to handle finances you will never be a leader."
~ **Bishop T.D. Jakes**

I was inspired to produce this book after hurricane Harvey flooded the city of Houston, TX in 2017. The hurricane hit the city of Corpus Christi first. Corpus Christi is a Spanish phrase that means "the body of Christ" in English. The resulting flood revealed that too many men in the body of Christ lacked the ability to take care of their families in an emergency due to financial illiteracy. GOD's men brought hardship and shame on their selves and their families because they were not prepared financially to respond properly to a flood emergency. They failed to build an ARK which is an acronym for Anointed Revelation Knowledge that would have helped them create a financial plan to survive a flood in a Gulf of Mexico area city that sits only 50 feet above sea level. I watched too many men being interviewed on TV in while sitting in shelters complaining that they didn't have any money to take care of their families independently. A George Washington University survey asked middle-class men how quickly could they raise $2,000 to meet an unexpected need. Only 40% of them could raise the money within 30 days.

"The fault, dear Brutus, is not in our stars, but in ourselves, that we are underlings." ~ **Cassius**

The one thing that keeps the average man living like an underling is financial illiteracy. Financial illiteracy is a disease that has crippled families for many generations. I say it is a disease because it spawns hatred, prejudice, and bigotry as people who struggle financially need to blame their failure on somebody. Each time America has a down turn in the economy we see a corresponding rise in racial hatred, prejudice, and bigotry. We should be furious with the politicians and business people who caused the economy to fall rather than each other. But the average person is uninformed so they don't know who to blame. No one seems smart enough to ask a simple question such as how can 50% of the American people be financially illiterate in a nation that runs on capitalism? Our living conditions, social status, transportation, access to justice, the food we eat, and so on are all dependent on the commodity called money that most people have no clue about how to manage properly.

When you understand there is a correlation between a lack of education and incarceration it won't be difficult to see that financial illiteracy can put your liberty in jeopardy. According to the FBI's Bureau of Criminal Justice Statistics over 70% of men in prison are there for money related crimes such as: robbery, burglary, fraud, extortion, larceny, and so on. The average factory worker makes about $1,200 a week but run out of money before the end of the week. People look shamefully at a person who is 60 that can't read but they never stop to think about how the world would view them if they knew they were illiterate financially. What if everyone knew you had no savings and no clue about how to manage money except for getting from paycheck to paycheck? In order to cure the disease of financial illiteracy people must be taught: how to save, control their cost of living, borrow money effectively, and diversify intelligently so they can have money working for them rather than them working for it. You can go to my website www.drwillspeaking.com and find resources to help you excel in these areas.

Getting money is one thing and keeping it is a whole other ball game. Men who are wealthy understand the rules of and how to play both games very well. There are three abilities you must have in order to obtain and retain wealth which are: lead, read, and visualize. Hosea 4:6 says my people are destroyed for a lack of knowledge. Over 65% of pro athletes file bankruptcy or end up with no money at the end of their careers due to a lack of knowledge or a high level of financial illiteracy. Most young men want to be wealthy, a celebrity, or a wealthy celebrity. However, they don't understand that financial literacy can make you wealthy, a celebrity, or a wealthy celebrity depending on what you do with what you learned. The real problem they have is their ego won't allow them to purchase the knowledge or make the investment to obtain financial literacy. They don't understand that learning inspires vision that helps lead us to our GOD ordained destiny where there is always wealth and prosperity.

Proverbs 29:18 says where there is no vision people perish. Wealthy men survive competition and other forces that try to drive them into bankruptcy because they are visionaries. Vision gives men the ability to see their enemies coming and to identify as well as take advantage of opportunities others have yet to recognize. Visionaries learn to use money as a tool and a seed. They spread their money around in 7 or 8 different growth investments so they will always have some growing when others have none. They understand that money is like manure. If you spread money around it will act like fertilizer and make whatever you put it into grow. But if you pile it up in one place it will stink.

"Cast your bread [re: money] upon the waters: for you shall find it after many days. Give a portion to seven, and also to eight; for you know not what evil shall be upon the earth (Ecclesiastes 11:1-2)."

Lastly, creating and managing wealth requires leadership. No man ever becomes wealthy alone. A lone wolf can become rich but he cannot be wealthy. A man who wants to be wealthy must have the ability to lead other people to want to help him obtain and retain wealth.

Men often reject financial literacy programs because they take too long to learn and are often too expensive. The reason it takes a long time is because the average man does not yet understand who he is, the mindset he is operating in, and he fights against facing the truth to make the necessary change. Knowing who you are, your mindset, and accepting the truth that the way you think is what led you to be where you are takes time for men to learn and properly adjust to. Also, we live in an age of immediate gratification. Therefore, most men don't have the patience to go through programs that take 5 to 10 years to master. The microwave generation wants to receive quick answers to long term problems.

In response to that need I wrote "Accessing New Covenant Wealth" so that men can receive the knowledge in it quickly and benefit from immediately. Yes, you can actually profit by applying this knowledge to your life, family, or business immediately. However, the huge gains you want won't come until you have worked the principles diligently everyday for 3 to 5 years. Intelligence is measured by the speed it takes you to recognize what you need to change. The only reason you are not wealthy right now is because of what you have been doing and the way you have been thinking. Those who have the intelligence to change what they do and the way they think quickly will reach the level of profitability more rapidly.

The men of GOD must change the way they have been taught to think about giving, tithing, and sacrificing in church. That mindset has led men to become voluntary victims of abuse mentally, spiritually, and financially. The Most High GOD does not want offerings and sacrifices like the pagan gods. In fact, the way we give offerings and sacrifices hoping to receive blessings as pagan worshippers do angers GOD. In Psalms 50 HE said: Hear, O my people, and I will speak; O Israel, and I will testify against you: I am GOD, even your GOD. I will not reprove you for your sacrifices or your burnt offerings, to have been continually before me. I will take no bullock out of your house or he goats out of your folds for every beast of the forest is mine, and the cattle upon a thousand hills… if I were hungry, I would not tell you for the world is mine and the fullness thereof… offer unto GOD thanksgiving; and pay your vows [keep your promises] unto the most High: and call upon me in the day of trouble: I will deliver you and you shall glorify me." The truth is this: the blessings of GOD come through the faith contained in the words you say before GOD and the things you do for others selflessly in the name of GOD.

The primary power point in this book is the understanding that every physical entity has a spiritual property. Every product or service you create is a physical entity but the way you extract the maximum value out of them is by understanding how to access the power contained in their spiritual property. Money is a form of spiritual power that hides inside every physical entity. Accessing that power is part of our New Covenant inheritance. However, we must understand how to access it. By the time you finish studying this book you will understand two things: 1) how to access New Covenant wealth; and 2) what has been blocking you from accessing it.

CHAPTER 1

QUALIFYING FOR THE NEW COVENANT

"…if any man be **in** Christ, he is a new creature: old things are passed away; behold, all things are become new (2Corinthians 5:17)."

"If so be that you have heard Him [Jesus] and have been taught by Him, as the truth is in Jesus: that you put off concerning the former conversation the old man, which is corrupt according to the deceitful lusts; and be renewed in the spirit of your mind; and that you put on the new man, which after GOD is created in righteousness and true holiness (Ephesians 4:21-24)."

If you are between the ages of 40 and 65 you are the children of the Civil Rights generation. You are also in the contemporary church demographic most likely to be praying to GOD for a breakthrough but can't figure out, with all the church going and seed sowing you do, why you haven't broken through. You can't understand why it seems GOD is withholding the promises of the New Covenant from you. Well, there are 3 primary reasons you have not broken through: 1) you have been led to believe that GOD is going to break you through. The truth is you must use the power GOD has given you to break through on your own. When it is time for a bird to break through its shell does GOD break her out? No, she has to peck her own way out; 2) you have been led to believe that sowing a seed will allow you to buy your way into the New Covenant abundance. Using natural things in order to gain access to or cause things of the spirit world to move is a type of witchcraft. It is what witches and warlocks like Simon the Sorcerer in Acts 8:18 would do; and 3) you are the offspring of people that GOD led out of Jim Crow era Egyptian like captivity who refused to go into the Promised Land but decided to integrate with Pharaoh.

Now, because of your age you are beginning to think that it's over for you. However GOD still wants to get the Egypt out of you and teach your mind to be free from the captivity of poverty so that you can be wealthy. But you must come out of Egypt's tradition of Babylonian religion and get the truth of the word of GOD **in** you so that you can be righteous. Matthew 6:33 says: seek first the kingdom of GOD and HIS righteousness, not religious righteousness, if you want the things of GOD to be added to you.

In order to be in righteousness with GOD you must reject what religion has taught you and "let this mind be in you which was also in Christ Jesus". Romans 8:7 says: the carnal mind is in opposition to GOD because it cannot adhere to the word of GOD. In order to cleanse your mind of carnality you must allow someone to flood your mind with the truth of the word of GOD in a process similar to pouring clear clean water into a glass of muddy water. As you pour more and more clean water in that glass more of the muddy water gets flushed out until it all becomes clean. You must be filled with the clean clear water of GOD's word in order to be in GOD's righteousness.

"Your word have I hid in my heart that I might not sin against you (Psalms 119:11)."

"GOD is a Spirit and they that worship HIM must worship HIM in spirit and in truth (John 4:24)."

"...the Lord said unto Moses: rise up early in the morning, stand before Pharaoh, and say unto him: thus said the Lord GOD of the Hebrews: Let my people go that they may serve me (Exodus 9:13)."

The Civil Rights generation has not been free to worship GOD in spirit and in truth because they were led through religion to compromise with Pharaoh. Instead of coming out of Egypt they decided to continue serving GOD in Egypt's Babylonian religious traditions. GOD wanted HIS people to separate from Pharaoh and go out into the wilderness, or outside of church, so HE could free their minds from Egypt's doctrines that served to keep them in mental and spiritual captivity. However, they passed on that opportunity and decided to integrate with Pharaoh in a voluntary captivity. It is said that what is past is prolog which means that which was done in the past serves to foretell the future. GOD is having a hard time trying to lead the Civil Rights generation era children into the Promised Land today because too many preachers are working to lead them back to Egypt

14

through Babylonian religious doctrines and traditions. GOD is also having difficulty leading non church going people to HIM because the so-called woke, conscious, and enlightened people are also leading them back to Egypt by worshiping Babylonian gods and goddesses.

The Old Testament serves as a school master to teach us not to do what the children of Israel did that caused them to fall out of favor with GOD. The Old Testament and Old Covenant are called "old" because there are no longer any rights and benefits that can be obtained from them. The New Testament children of GOD can access the rights and benefits of the New Covenant by being righteous or in right standing with the principles written by GOD in the New Testament.

A testament is called a will because it documents the inheritance a person wants their children to receive upon their death. The New Testament documents what GOD wanted HIS children to receive upon the death of HIS son Jesus. Once a new will has been written the old will is no longer valid. That means you cannot receive the inheritance or any of the covenant rights and benefits from the old will or old covenant because there is a new will and a New Covenant. A covenant is a type of performance contract that outlines the provisions one is entitled to receive for proper contract performance. If we adhere to the performance requirements of the New Testament which are: believe that Jesus is the son of GOD and that GOD has raised Him from the dead we are eligible then to receive an inheritance from the New Covenant.

Now, there is a difference between being eligible and qualified. Everyone who is eligible is not qualified. If there are actions you commit that cause you to become disqualified, you lose all access to the covenant rights and benefits. The average church going Christian is being denied access to their New Covenant inheritance because their preachers are leading them to try to access the New Testament rights and benefits by following Old Testament law. If you are a Christian who is determined to never sin, the devil doesn't have to make you sin he only needs to lead you to follow the law. If he leads you to follow the law, you will sin because no one can keep the law. The devil can destroy the diehard church going Christian then by simply leading them to become subject to the curse of the law.

"And the Lord's anger was kindled against Israel, and HE made them wander in the wilderness forty years, until all the generation, that had done evil in the sight of the Lord, was consumed. And, behold, you are risen up in your fathers' stead, an increase of sinful men, to augment yet the fierce anger of the Lord toward Israel (Numbers 32:14-15)."

GOD is waiting for the Civil Rights generation of parents to pass away before their children will be allowed to enter the New Testament Promised Land. These parents refuse to give up their old time religion that leads them to worship their pastor more than GOD which makes him an idol or a type of Babylonian god. The first thing we must do to regain access to our New Covenant rights and benefits is to have a conversation about how to break out of the captivity of Babylonian religion that is practiced in every church every week. We must cast the spirit of Babylon out of the house of GOD so that GOD's people can be free from the curse of the law. GOD will not allow HIS children to receive their inheritance of power, wealth, and riches from the kingdom of GOD as long as they are still unwittingly worshipping idol gods. People who try to make excuses like "GOD knows my heart" so they can be disobedient and keep their tradition of worshipping idol gods need to know that GOD doesn't make any exceptions to HIS rules.

"For this you know, that **no** whoremonger, nor unclean person, nor covetous man, who is an **idolater**, has **any inheritance** in the kingdom of Christ and of GOD. Let no man deceive you with vain words: for because of **these** things comes the wrath of GOD upon the children of disobedience. Be not you therefore partakers with them for you were sometimes darkness, but now are you light in the Lord: walk as children of light... proving what is acceptable unto the Lord. And have no fellowship with the unfruitful works of darkness, but rather reprove them (Ephesians 5:5-11)."

Hopefully the conversation we are going to have through this book will cause conversion out of idolatry and the tradition of Babylonian worship in church. We must seek GOD's righteousness as HE outlined in the New Testament. Unless we are converted from the idolatry of Babylon into the righteousness of the Most High GOD we cannot have access to the rights and benefits of HIS New Covenant. Until we make the conversion into Christ likeness we will not become heirs to the kingdom. Idolaters are not eligible to share in the commonwealth of Israel, enter the treasure room of heaven, or receive an inheritance through the riches of the kingdom of GOD.

"But I have prayed for you that your faith fail not: and when you are converted strengthen your brethren (Luke 22:32)."

A person can be converted more easily by understanding what they value and why. The average person values money and celebrity because everything they see on secular and Christian TV entices them to lust for wealth and fame. Once you discover what people value you can engage them in conversation. Conversation creates conversion. The easiest way to convert a person to Christ Jesus is by having heart to heart conversations with them where you are listening more than talking.

Church leaders are coming to understand that we cannot use the old religious approach to convert new people. But they have gone too far by bringing too much of the world into church. Older Christians are waging the battle for new converts but we are losing the war because people are coming into church but not out of the world. They are getting saved but few are converting into new life in Christ Jesus. Therefore, we must jump off the hamster wheel of our insanity, be more attentive, and become more conversational by talking with not to or at people. Converting a person from the world does not require you or me to become worldly. We only need to do 3 things: stop for them, talk to them, and touch them. Listen to where they want to go and let them know you have the knowledge and resources to help them reach their goals.

CHAPTER 2

KEYS TO THE COVENANT (PART 1)

"And I will give unto you the keys of the kingdom of heaven: and whatsoever you shall bind on earth shall be bound in heaven: and whatsoever you shall loose on earth shall be loosed in heaven (Matthew 16:19)."

GOD prescribed a New Covenant because we could not adhere to the laws of the Old Covenant. In order to empower us to remain in covenant with HIM GOD created a New Covenant that made us joint-heirs to the throne of grace with Christ Jesus. The New Covenant also made us eligible to receive an inheritance of abundance through the riches of the Kingdom of GOD.

But, as a result of the doctrines and traditions of religion we have not obtained access to the benefits of the New Covenant because the keys we need to open the door have not been revealed to us. If you don't know where you are going, without divine guidance you will never know when you've arrived. Conversely, you will never know you've arrived if you don't know where you are going or how to get there. The place where we need to arrive to access the benefits of the

New Covenant is the Kingdom of GOD. The way that we get there is by divine guidance or by faith through grace in righteousness.

Hosea 4:6 says "my people are destroyed for a lack of knowledge" and Proverbs 4:7 says "in all of your getting get understanding". The average born again Christian has been deprived of the benefits of the New Covenant because we have not been taught the proper knowledge and understanding of the primary keys that we need to enter and remain in that covenant. Jesus said in Matthew 16:19 I will give you the keys to the kingdom of GOD and whatsoever you bind and loose on earth will be bound and loosed in heaven. Those keys that GOD promised to give you are: understanding what righteousness, faith, grace, and the Kingdom of GOD actually are. With that understanding we can unlock the door to the treasure room of heaven.

Ironically, we have been bound on earth without the keys to get loose because we do not have the definitions GOD intended to convey when HE uses those words. Using the wrong definition takes away their power to loose or unlock the treasure room of heaven and keeps us from gaining access to new covenant wealth. The definitions of the words: righteousness, faith, grace and the kingdom of GOD are only abstract concepts to most Christians. The commonly held definitions of those words do not provide a true understanding which is why their meanings change depending on which preacher you talk to and what denomination he belongs to. Therefore, we must learn the TRUE definitions that provide a concrete understanding of what they mean rather than an abstract concept. Then, we will understand how to utilize those words as keys to unlock the door to the New Covenant treasury **room**.

• **Faith** – as conveyed in the mind of the True and Living GOD has two primary definitions: 1) the word of GOD; and 2) Jesus; Hebrews 11:6 says: without faith it is impossible to please GOD but what GOD was intending to convey is that without Jesus it is impossible to please HIM.

• **Grace** – the word grace, depending on the context in which it is used, means power, the power of GOD, or the power of GOD acting on behalf of the believer. All of that nonsense about grace being an unmerited favor was designed by the devil's disciples to create confusion for the purpose of robbing you of the opportunity to have the power of GOD to operating in your life.

• **Righteousness** – means to be in right standing with GOD

• **Kingdom of GOD** – is an economic system through which GOD provides provision to HIS people on earth; it is NOT the place where GOD resides.

Now, we need to study each of these words in depth so you can understand how to use them to unlock your rights and benefits in the New Covenant. It's important to remember the reason GOD provided a New Covenant is so that we can be free from the curse of the Old

Covenant and to receive our full rights and benefits as HIS sons rather that HIS servants. Galatians 4:21-26 Galatians explains rather plainly that the old covenant was given to men who were born in bondage to a woman of bondage. A woman of bondage in the Bible is an allegory of the old covenant because it leads men to practice religion. Religion is a form of bondage that keeps us out of righteousness, cursed, and in constant conflict with GOD.

"Tell me, you that desire to be under the law, do you not hear the law? For it is written, that Abraham had two sons, the one by a bondmaid, the other by a freewoman. But he who was of the bondwoman was born after the flesh; but he of the freewoman was by promise. These things are an allegory: for these are the two covenants; the one from the Mount Sinai, which gender to bondage, which is Hagar. For this Hagar is Mount Sinai in Arabia, and answers to Jerusalem which now is, and is in bondage with her children. But Jerusalem which is above is free, which is the mother of us all (Galatians 4:21-26)."

When you read further you will see that Galatians 4:28-31 says the children of the bondwoman could not be heirs with the children of promise. The people who are in bondage to religion will always persecute the children of promise. The truth of the word conflicts with the children of the bondwoman's religious doctrine and traditions. Being the Great Father HE is GOD issued a new covenant to free the children of promise from the bondage of religion, the curse of the law,

23

and to lead us into peace and prosperity with HIM. I just paraphrased those verses in Galatians so here is what they actually say:

"Now we, brethren, as Isaac was, are the children of promise. But as then he that was born after the flesh persecuted him that was born after the Spirit, even so as it is now. Nevertheless what says the scripture? Cast out the bondwoman and her son: for the son of the bondwoman shall not be heir with the son of the freewoman. So then, brothers, we are not children of the bondwoman but of the free (Galatians 4:28-31)."

Those who are children of the free woman are no longer subject to the law. We are heirs to the new covenant promises and can obtain access to the new covenant wealth and riches. But in order to obtain that access we must first cast out the bondwoman or cast out religious practices so that we can be in right standing with GOD and be free from the curse of the law. Secondly, we must have a true understanding of how to access new covenant wealth and riches by faith, through grace, in righteousness. So, let's study the words faith, grace, righteousness, and the phrase: kingdom of GOD in depth. Then you will understand what the kingdom of GOD is as it relates to new covenant wealth and riches and why faith, grace, and righteousness are the keys that unlock the entrance to it.

New Covenant Keys

Key #1 – the Kingdom of GOD

24

In Luke 17:20-21 Jesus said: The kingdom of GOD will not come with observation because the kingdom of GOD is within you. And the Apostle Paul said in 1 Corinthians 4:20 that the kingdom of GOD is not in word but in power. These verses provide evidence that the kingdom of GOD is not a location. The Kingdom of Heaven is the place where GOD resides. The kingdom of GOD is the economic system that the Kingdom of Heaven operates on. America is the place where we reside. Capitalism is the economic system that America operates on. When GOD wants to deliver provisions to HIS children HE does it through the system of the kingdom of GOD.

GOD gives you a provision of money for two reasons: to meet your needs and to fulfill your purpose. A good father doesn't just provide he also sustains. Therefore, GOD provides you with subsistence until you learn how to receive abundance. Deuteronomy 8:18 says GOD has given you power to get wealth. The only stipulation HE placed on you getting wealth is you must get it through HIS system of provision which is what the Bible calls the "Kingdom of GOD". We've been having difficulty getting money because no one ever taught us that the spiritual energy or ideas that lead to cash comes through Heaven's economic system of distribution and supply.

It is important for you to understand that the Kingdom of Heaven and the kingdom of GOD are two different things. The Kingdom of Heaven is the place where GOD resides. The kingdom of GOD is the economic system that Heaven operates on. When you have Christ "in" you it gives you the power or authority to access the riches of kingdom of GOD or the common wealth of Israel by Christ Jesus. This is why Jesus said the kingdom of GOD is in you, where your heart is there will be your treasure also, and why the Apostle Paul said the kingdom of GOD comes by or through power or like Ephesians 3:20 says: according to the power that is working in you. Therefore, one of the ways to access your rights and benefits of the New Covenant is by using the power of GOD in you to enter the kingdom of GOD by or through faith which is a euphemism for Jesus or Christ in you.

Key #2 – Faith

John 1:1-3 tells us that in the beginning was the Word, and the Word was with GOD, and the Word was GOD. The same was in the beginning with GOD. All things were made by Him; and without Him was not anything made that was made. Based on this scripture we know that the name Jesus is synonymous with the word of GOD. But we also need to know that the name Jesus is also synonymous with the word faith. The word faith is simply a euphemism for Jesus.

We've been taught faith as an abstract concept. Nobody has a concrete grasp on what faith actually is. Like 5 year olds we've been conditioned to respond to the question what is faith by saying: it's the substance of things hoped for but that definition still does not tell you what faith actually is. Our lack of understanding on what faith really is has denied us access to the truth and power contained in the word of GOD. Through religious doctrine and tradition the devil threw a veil over the true meaning of faith to prevent us from obtaining and using the power that comes with having dominion and authority. In the process he also blocked our access to our own New Covenant rights and benefits. Faith is Jesus, Jesus is the word of GOD, Jesus and the word of GOD are one, therefore faith is also the word of GOD. So, whenever you see the word faith in the Bible you can exchange it for either the name of Jesus or the phrase "the word of GOD" and it will bring greater clarity to that verse's meaning immediately. Let's study **Galatians 3:1-29** verse by verse to see how GOD used the word faith while explaining to us the futility in trying to keep the law.

"O foolish Galatians, who has bewitched you, that you should not obey the truth, before whose eyes Jesus Christ has been evidently set forth, crucified among you?

² This only would I learn of you: received you the Spirit by the works of the law, or by the hearing of faith? [He said: did you receive the Holy Spirit by the law or by hearing Jesus; by hearing the word of GOD?]

³ Are you so foolish? Having begun in the Spirit, are you now made perfect by the flesh?

⁴ Have you suffered so many things in vain?

⁵ He therefore that minister to you the Spirit, and work miracles among you, doeth he it by the works of the law, or by the hearing of faith? [He is saying it had to be by Jesus]

⁶ Even as Abraham believed GOD, and it was accounted to him for righteousness.

⁷ Know you therefore that they which are of faith, the same are the children of Abraham.

⁸ And the scripture, foreseeing that GOD would justify the heathen through faith [Jesus], preached before the gospel [of the New Covenant] unto Abraham, saying, in you shall all nations be blessed.

⁹ So then they which be of faith [Jesus] are blessed with faithful Abraham.

¹⁰ For as many as are of the works of the law are under the curse: for it is written, Cursed is every one that continues not in all things which are written in the book of the law to do them [Now you should understand why so many things have been going wrong in your body, life, and community. When we follow the law, whether knowingly or unknowingly, it makes us subject to the curse or penalty of the law that causes all kinds of maladies and calamities].

¹¹ But that no man is justified by the law in the sight of GOD, it is evident: for, the just shall live by faith [Jesus] [you see, the law required you to give sacrificial offerings, but sacrificial offerings under grace, where you should be living by faith, brings a curse.]

¹²And the law is not of faith [Jesus]: but, the man that do them shall live in them [he who is hell bent on following the law must live in the law because if he breaks one law he broke them all.]

¹³Christ has redeemed us from the curse of the law, being made a curse for us: for it is written, cursed is every one that hangs on a tree: [people who worshiped tress hung their faith on trees; this is where the Christmas tree came from. GOD is trying to get you down off of that tree and lead you to get Jesus of the cross which is made from trees.]

¹⁴[So] that the blessing of Abraham might come on the Gentiles through Jesus Christ; that we might receive the promise of the Spirit through faith [Jesus].

¹⁵Brethren, I speak after the manner of men; though it be but a man's covenant, yet if it be confirmed, no man disannuls or adds thereto.

¹⁶Now to Abraham and his seed were the [New Covenant] promises made. He said not, and to seeds, as of many; but as of one, and to your seed, which is Christ [do you see that the only seed that GOD made available for you to sow to receive blessings is Christ in you, not money in church?]

¹⁷And this I say, that the [old] covenant, that was confirmed before of GOD in Christ, the law, which was four hundred and thirty years after, cannot disannul, that it should make the [New Covenant] promise of none effect [the Apostle Paul is teaching us that the new

covenant was promised to Abraham 430 years before the law came but the law did not annul GOD's promise. If you really understand what Paul said here, you should be dancing out of your socks.]

[18] For if the inheritance be of the law, it is no more of promise: but GOD gave it to Abraham by promise [before HE gave Moses the law].

[19] Wherefore then serves the law [OK, now, this is why GOD instituted the law…]? It was added because of transgressions, **till the seed** [or until Jesus] **should come** [to the seed of Abraham] **to whom the promise was made;** and it was ordained by angels in the hand of a mediator.

[20] Now a mediator is not a mediator of one, but GOD is one.

[21] Is the law then against the promises of GOD? GOD forbid: for if there had been a law given which could have given life, verily righteousness should have been by the law.

[22] But the scripture has concluded all under sin that the promise by faith of Jesus Christ might be given to them that believe.

[23] But before faith [Jesus] came, we were kept under the law, shut up unto the faith [or locked away from the power of the word of GOD] which should afterwards be revealed.

[24] **Wherefore the law was our schoolmaster to bring us unto Christ**, that we might be justified by faith [Jesus].

²⁵ <u>But after that faith is come,</u> [after Jesus came] we are no longer under a schoolmaster [or subject to the law].

²⁶ For you are all the children of GOD by faith [or by the word of GOD] in Christ Jesus.

²⁷ For as many of you as have been baptized into Christ have put on Christ [that means].

²⁸ There is neither Jew nor Greek, there is neither bond nor free, there is neither male nor female: for you are all one in Christ Jesus.

²⁹ **And if you be Christ's, then are you Abraham's seed, and heirs [to an inheritance from the kingdom of GOD] according to the promise.**

So, if you take nothing else away from this lesson remember: faith is NOT the substance of things hoped for. Jesus is the substance of things hoped for. The word of GOD is the substance of things hoped for. If the word of GOD says you can have it, by the power of GOD you can get it. Jesus is the evidence of things not seen because He is the word of GOD. Jesus fulfilled all Bible prophecy. Whatever it says He would do He did. Therefore, Jesus is the evidence or proof that everything the Bible says exists in the spirit realm is real. If Jesus gave you a promise, His word is the evidence or proof that He will deliver it.

"…a woman of Canaan came out of the same coasts, and cried unto Him [Jesus], saying, have mercy on me, O Lord, son of David; my daughter is grievously vexed with a devil. But He answered her not a word. And his disciples came and besought him, saying: send her away; for she cries after us. But He answered and said, I am not sent but unto the lost sheep of the house of Israel. Then came she and worshipped Him, saying, Lord, help me. But he answered and said, it is not meet to take the children's bread, and to cast it to dogs. And she said, truth, Lord: yet the dogs eat of the crumbs which fall from their masters' table. Then Jesus answered and said unto her, O woman, great is your faith [or understanding of my word]: be it unto you even as you will. And her daughter was made whole from that very hour (Matthew 15:2-28)."

You see, the Syrophenician woman was able to get in on a blessing that belonged to the children of GOD which she was not entitled to receive but she obtained access to it, by or through her understanding of faith, Jesus, or the word of GOD.

Now, let's use Hebrews 11 to further prove your new definition of faith and you will discover the truth of who Jesus is and how He operates has been hidden from you. There is no such thing as a first or second coming of Jesus. He walked with ALL the people of GOD from the beginning of time supplying them with power and meeting their every need. This is why He promised us in Matthew 28:20 that He would be with us "alway" meaning: all the way; from beginning to end. If you follow along in your King James Version of the Bible, every place where the word "faith" appears, I am going to replace it with either the name Jesus or the phrase: the word of GOD.

Hebrews

Chapter 11

Now faith [Jesus] is the substance of things hoped for, the evidence of things not seen.

² For by it [Jesus] the elders obtained a good report.

³ Through faith [the word of GOD in John 1:1-3] we understand that the worlds were framed by the word of GOD [Jesus], so that things which are seen were not made of things which do appear.

⁴ By faith [Jesus] Abel offered unto GOD a more excellent sacrifice than Cain, by which he obtained witness that he was righteous, GOD testifying of his gifts: and by it he being dead yet speaks.

⁵ By faith [Jesus] Enoch was translated that he should not see death; and was not found, because GOD had translated him: for before his translation he had this testimony, that he pleased GOD.

⁶ But without faith [Jesus] it is impossible to please GOD: for he that comes to GOD must believe that HE is, and that HE rewards them that diligently seek him.

[7] By faith [Jesus] Noah, being warned of GOD of things not seen as yet, moved with fear, prepared an ark to the saving of his house; by the which he condemned the world, and became heir of the righteousness which is by faith[Jesus].

[8] By faith [Jesus] Abraham, when he was called to go out into a place which he should after receive for an inheritance, obeyed; and he went out, not knowing whither he went.

[9] By faith [Jesus] he sojourned in the land of promise, as in a strange country, dwelling in tabernacles with Isaac and Jacob, the heirs with him of the same promise:

[10] For he looked for a city which has foundations, whose builder and maker is GOD.

[11] Through faith [Jesus] also Sara herself received strength [or power] to conceive seed, and was delivered of a child when she was past age, because she judged him faithful who had promised.

[12] Therefore sprang there even of one, and him as good as dead, so many as the stars of the sky in multitude, and as the sand which is by the sea shore innumerable.

[13] These all died in faith [in Jesus], not having received the promises, but having seen them afar off, and were persuaded of them, and embraced them, and confessed that they were strangers and pilgrims on the earth.

¹⁴ For they that say such things declare plainly that they seek a country.

¹⁵ And truly, if they had been mindful of that country from whence they came out, they might have had opportunity to have returned.

¹⁶ But now they desire a better country that is heavenly: wherefore GOD is not ashamed to be called their GOD: for he has prepared for them a city.

¹⁷ By faith [Jesus] Abraham, when he was tried, offered up Isaac: and he that had received the promises offered up his only begotten son,

¹⁸ Of whom it was said, that in Isaac shall your seed be called:

¹⁹ Accounting that GOD was able to raise him up, even from the dead; from whence also he received him in a figure.

²⁰ By faith [the word of GOD] Isaac blessed Jacob and Esau concerning things to come.

²¹ By faith [the word of GOD] Jacob, when he was a dying, blessed both the sons of Joseph; and worshipped, leaning upon the top of his staff.

²² By faith [the word of GOD] Joseph, when he died, made mention of the departing of the children of Israel; and gave commandment concerning his bones.

[23] By faith [Jesus] Moses, when he was born, was hid three months of his parents, because they saw he was a proper child; and they were not afraid of the king's commandment.

[24] By faith [Jesus] Moses, when he was come to years, refused to be called the son of Pharaoh's daughter;

[25] Choosing rather to suffer affliction with the people of GOD, than to enjoy the pleasures of sin for a season;

[26] Esteeming the reproach of Christ greater riches than the treasures in Egypt: for he had respect unto the recompence of the reward.

[27] By faith [the word of GOD] he forsook Egypt, not fearing the wrath of the king: for he endured, as seeing him who is invisible.

[28] Through faith [the word of GOD] he kept the Passover, and the sprinkling of blood, lest he that destroyed the firstborn should touch them.

[29] By faith [Jesus] they passed through the Red sea as by dry land: which the Egyptians assaying to do were drowned.

[30] By faith [Jesus] the walls of Jericho fell down, after they were compassed about seven days.

[31] By faith [Jesus] the harlot Rahab perished not with them that believed not, when she had received the spies with peace.

³² And what shall I more say? for the time would fail me to tell of Gedeon, and of Barak, and of Samson, and of Jephthae; of David also, and Samuel, and of the prophets:

³³ Who through faith subdued kingdoms, wrought righteousness, obtained promises, stopped the mouths of lions.

³⁴ Quenched the violence of fire, escaped the edge of the sword, out of weakness were made strong, waxed valiant in fight, turned to flight the armies of the aliens.

³⁵ Women received their dead raised to life again: and others were tortured, not accepting deliverance; that they might obtain a better resurrection...

³⁹ And these all, having obtained a good report through faith [or through Jesus], received not the promise [but]:

⁴⁰ **GOD having provided some better thing for us, that they without us should not be made perfect.**

CHAPTER 3

KEYS TO THE COVENANT (PART 2)

"You cannot think on a level that is higher than what you've been exposed to." ~ **Van Moody**

Jesus Lives

In order to have strong and powerful faith we must believe that GOD is and that Jesus lives. If you begin in Genesis and you know how to identify Jesus in the word, you will be able to follow Jesus' life all the way through the Bible to the book of revelation. You will see He appeared to help or teach many men at various times throughout history in the flesh or in a physical body. Chili con carne is a Spanish phrase that means: Chili with meat. Carne means meat or flesh. Carne is the base word of the word "reincarnation" which means: to be in the flesh again.

The agents of satan in religion will label you as a lunatic if you talk about the many incarnations of Jesus because they don't want you to believe in the resurrection. Your mind has to be exposed to a high level of Bible intelligence in order for your thinking to break free from worldly and religious captivity. When we teach about reincarnation as it is presented in the Bible, of course, we are not talking about people coming back to life as insects or animals. We are talking about Jesus coming back in a physical body or in the flesh. If you the world or religious leaders to ridicule you into believing there is no such thing as reincarnation then you will let them bully you into denying the principle premise of your Christian belief system which is Jesus lives!

There were many instances where Jesus raised other people from the dead or brought them back to life in the flesh or in their physical bodies before and after his own resurrection:

"And the graves were opened; and **many** bodies of the saints which slept arose, and came **out** of the **graves** after His [Jesus'] resurrection, and went into the holy city, and appeared unto many (Matthew 27:52-53)."

"And when He [Jesus] thus had spoken, He cried with a loud voice, Lazarus, come forth. And he that was **dead** came forth, bound hand and foot with grave clothes: and his face was bound about with a napkin. Jesus said to them: loose him, and let him go (John 11:43-44)."

Psalms 46:1 says: "GOD is our refuge and strength, a very **present** help in trouble" which means Jesus will actually show up when you really need Him as HE did for the 3 Hebrew boys who refused to bow down before an idol god and was thrown in a furnace to be burned to death:

"Then Nebuchadnezzar the king was astonished, and rose up in haste, and spoke, and said to his counselors: did not we cast three men bound into the midst of the fire? They answered and said to the king: true, O king. He answered and said: lo, I see four men loose, walking in the midst of the fire, and they have no hurt; and the form of the fourth is like the Son of GOD (Daniel 3:24-25)."

Do you see Jesus was walking in the midst of the fire with the 3 Hebrew boys? It shouldn't be hard then for you to see and accept as truth that Jesus appeared to his disciples 13 times AFTER the resurrection to teach us that we also have the ability to come back in the flesh. Jesus is our preeminent or first example in all things. Whatever we have seen Him do we can do also. After His resurrection Jesus appeared to 11 of the disciples when Thomas was not there and another time when Thomas was present. When Jesus stood on the shore in John 21:5 and asked the disciples as they were fishing: do you have any meat, that incident also occurred after His resurrection. And in verse 14 it says: "This is now the third time that Jesus showed Himself to His disciples, **after** He had risen from the dead."

In Acts 1:1-3 the Apostle Paul said: "The former treatise have I made, O Theophilus, of all that Jesus began both to do and teach until the day in which He was taken up, after that He through the Holy Ghost had given commandments unto the apostles whom He had chosen: to whom also He showed Himself _alive_ **after** His passion by **many** infallible proofs, being seen of them **forty days**, and speaking of the things pertaining to the kingdom of GOD. Finally, in 1 Corinthians 15:3-8 the Apostle Paul said:

"For I delivered unto you first of all that which I also received, how that Christ died for our sins according to the scriptures; and that He was buried, and that He rose again the third day according to the scriptures: and that He was seen of Cephas [or Peter], then of the twelve: after that, He was seen of above **five hundred brethren at once**; of whom the greater part remain unto this present, but some are fallen asleep. After that, He was seen of James; then of **all** the apostles. And last of all He was seen of me also, as of one born out of due time."

Can you see now why Hebrews 11 says Jesus is the evidence of things not seen? He is proof that whatever GOD says exists in the spirit world can materialize in the physical world.

"So then faith comes by hearing, and hearing by the word of GOD (Romans 10:17)."

"To whom GOD would make known what is the riches of the glory of this mystery among the Gentiles; which is Christ in you, the hope of glory (Colossians 1:27)."

The word "hearing" in Romans 10:17 comes from the Greek word "akouo" which means: to understand. We know now that faith is synonymous with Jesus therefore Romans 10:17 is saying: So then Jesus comes by understanding, and understanding by or through the word of GOD. The mystery of the riches of GOD's glory, according

41

to Colossians 1:27, is revealed in those who have allowed Christ Jesus to live in them. The way Christ Jesus comes to live in us is through understanding the word of GOD. If you remember that faith is Jesus and faith is the word of GOD, your faith will be alive and powerful when you allow Jesus to live incarnate or inside of you and you let His word work in you! Amen.

Increasing Your Faith

According to religious wisdom you can increase your faith by having more experiences with GOD and Jesus. In reality, having a greater number of experiences or proofs of GOD and Jesus' fidelity only increases your capacity to believe. Faith and belief are two different things. You don't need faith to believe. The primary way GOD intended you to obtain more faith is by increasing the volume and depth of the word of GOD that is living and working in you.

Romans 12:3 says: GOD has given every man a measure of faith. This tells us that every baby is born with a small measure of the word of GOD already in them. Contrary to popular belief babies are not born with an empty brain. Like a new computer they come with an operating program already installed. Babies come into the world with a sense of morality as well as right and wrong due to the word that was written in their hearts before they were born. When someone presents more of the word to them externally their spirit tells them it is true when it connects to the word they already have internally.

42

Faith or the word of GOD increases as you study the word and the depth and volume of the word that is working in you expands. You can read the word for 80 years but if you never study it your depth and volume will never expand or increase. In Mark 4:14-20 Jesus taught a parable designed to illustrate that when the word has no depth in your heart the storms of life and the cares of this world will steal or dilute the power of the word you received. 2 Timothy 2:15 teaches that we show ourselves approved of GOD by studying the word of GOD in order to rightly divide it in an effort to peer into its depths. According to Ephesians 3:20 the ability of GOD to do things for you is dependent on the power of the word that you have working in you. Your volume of the word of GOD increases on a linear plane as you study expansively to recognize the length and breadth of the word of GOD. That is, just how far the word of GOD has the ability to reach the entire world. Your depth of the word and power increases the more you study and dig deeper.

There are 4 levels or depths of the word of GOD that are described in the Greek language as:

Gnosis - meaning knowledge

Ginosko – intimate knowledge or wisdom

Epiginosko – to know fully or understand

43

Synesis – intelligence, secret knowledge, big picture, to see how everything works. You must have a security clearance to gain access to this level or depth of the word of GOD.

The 4 depths of Bible comprehension are: knowledge, wisdom, understanding, and intelligence. These depths are what the Apostle Paul was referring to in Ephesians 3:10 about the "manifold wisdom of GOD". Obtaining knowledge, wisdom, and understanding of the word of GOD is the process of learning everyone must go through to achieve abundance. Intelligence however is secret compartmented information that is revealed on a need to know basis. In Luke 8:10 Jesus told His disciples: unto you it is given to know the mysteries of the kingdom of GOD but to others in parables; that seeing they might not see and hearing they might not understand. This is why the Apostle Paul prayed in Ephesians 3:14-20: "for this cause I bow my knees unto the Father of our Lord Jesus Christ, of whom the whole family in heaven and earth is named, that He would grant you... to be able to comprehend with all saints what is the breadth, and length, and depth, and height; and to know the love of Christ, which passes knowledge, that you might be filled with all the fullness of GOD. Now unto Him that is able to do exceeding abundantly above all that we ask or think, according to the power that works in us."

There is tremendous power contained in simply knowing the word of GOD in that it empowers you to change your world by simply speaking it. Your power will increase as you dive deeper into the levels of intimate wisdom and full understanding. You obtain the power to operate in dominion and authority over this world at the level of synesis. Once you have been faith full to study diligently enough to reach the level of synesis GOD knows HE can trust you with intelligence and reveal HIS secret knowledge so you can see how everything works.

The reason the Apostle Paul was chosen, although he was killing Christians, is he had a zeal for GOD and he had already studied diligently enough to reach the synesis level but in his pre Christ state of mind GOD could not give him access to that power. Once GOD retrained his mind and mission from killing Christians to serving them HE could allow Paul to see the hidden mysteries of the word of GOD. The hidden knowledge of GOD is what satan really wants because at that depth is where the power to reign over the world resides. Therefore, GOD used the redemption of the Apostle Paul to show satan that redemption is possible for him if he would simply repent. GOD also used Paul to show you that even though you were acting as GOD's greatest enemy, going around sinning all willy-nilly, HE can redeem you too and transform you from pitiful to powerful by faith, by Jesus, or through the word of GOD.

Now let's look at grace with the understanding that it is the first gift of the New Covenant because the New Covenant ushered in the dispensation of grace. The New Covenant is where GOD has dispensed HIS power for us to operate in dominion and authority.

45

Therefore, grace is the primary key whereby we gain entrance to the treasure room of heaven or kingdom of GOD.

Grace

GOD intended for men to operate in dominion and authority in the earth as well as to operate as kings and priests in our homes. However, no man can operate effectively in dominion and authority without power. Under the Old Covenant where man was still vacillating in and out of sin under the law GOD could not trust men to have access to HIS power. Under the New Covenant men who are saved and in righteousness by Christ Jesus are one with GOD through Christ and can therefore be trusted with GOD's power. It was through GOD's power that you were saved and it is by GOD's power that you have the power to rule and reign over the earth in dominion and authority.

It is also through grace or the power of GOD that we rule or take dominion and authority over the system of the kingdom of GOD. You see, the devil has been fighting the people of GOD to steal our inheritance because he really wanted our power. We have been getting our butts kicked in the process because we don't know how to utilize our grace or power to fight him and win. This is why Matthew 11:12 says: the kingdom of GOD suffers [or allows] violence and the violent take it by force. Therefore, we must learn to use the violence or force of the grace or power of GOD to take and retain dominion and authority over the kingdom of GOD.

So, grace is NOT some mysterious unmerited favor. That definition is abstract and ambiguous because it does NOT actually tell you what that favor is and why it's unmerited. Depending on the religion or denomination the people you ask to define it adhere to you will get several different versions of what that favor is. That is because there is chaos and confusion involved in religion which is a system of bondage and captivity not one that generates truth. The truth will always make you free not keep you bound in confusion. Therefore, grace as GOD defines it is power, the power of GOD, or the power of GOD acting on behalf of the believer. Ephesians 2:5 & 8 says: by grace or by the power of GOD acting on your behalf you were saved.

If we study Ephesians Chapter 2 closely, it reveals the multitude of favors the grace or power of GOD has done for you. Beginning in verse 4 it says:

"But GOD, who is rich in mercy, for HIS great love wherewith HE loved us,

⁵ Even when we were dead in sins, has quickened us together with Christ, (**by grace you are saved**) [*or by HIS power acting on your behalf GOD gave you salvation*]

⁶ And has raised us up together, and made us sit together in heavenly places in Christ Jesus [or gave you a seat on the throne of grace]:

⁷ That in the ages to come HE might show the exceeding riches of HIS grace in HIS kindness toward us through Christ Jesus [*GOD gave you access to the treasury of heaven*].

⁸ For **by grace are you saved through faith** [Jesus]; and that not of yourselves: it is the gift of GOD:

⁹ Not of works lest any man should boast.

¹⁰ For we are HIS workmanship, created in Christ Jesus unto good works, which GOD has before ordained that we should walk in them [*gave you a purpose to fulfill*].

¹¹ Wherefore remember, that you being in time past Gentiles in the flesh, who are called un-circumcision by that which is called the Circumcision in the flesh made by hands;

¹² That at that time you were without Christ, being aliens from the **common/**<u>wealth</u> of Israel [*meaning you had no inheritance in Christ Jesus*], and strangers from the covenants of promise, having no hope, and without GOD in the world:

¹³ But now in Christ Jesus you who sometimes were far off are made nigh by the blood of Christ.

¹⁴ For He is our peace, who has made both one, and has broken down the middle wall of partition between us [*GOD gave you the blood of Jesus to cover your sins*];

¹⁵ Having abolished in his flesh the enmity, even the law of commandments contained in ordinances; for to make in Himself of twain one new man, so making peace [GOD *also gave you righteousness*]

The Law Blocks Access to the New Covenant

"And now, Israel, what does the Lord your GOD require of you, but to fear the Lord your GOD, to walk in all HIS ways, and to love HIM, and to serve the Lord your GOD with all your heart and with all your soul, to keep the commandments of the Lord, and HIS statutes, which I command you this day for your good (Deuteronomy 10:12-13)."

"But now we are delivered from the law, that being dead wherein we were held; that we should serve in newness of spirit, and not in the oldness of the letter. What shall we say then? Is the law sin? GOD forbid; no, I had not known sin, but by the law: for I had not known lust, except the law had said: Thou shall not covet. But sin, taking occasion [or advantage of us] by the commandment [GOD gave us to be fruitful and multiply], wrought in me all manner of concupiscence [spiritual and physical fornication] (Romans 7:6-8)."

The main thing that prevents you from accessing the riches of the kingdom of GOD after a lack of knowledge is a lack of righteousness. The one thing that prevents you from being righteous is sin. The law was originally given to us so that we could know when we were out of righteousness with GOD. Now that GOD has made a covenant of grace with man continuing to adhere to old covenant law puts us out of righteousness with GOD. GOD gave us grace or HIS power as a show of mercy to deliver us from the law because no man could keep the law. Therefore, many are still suffering due to following the law as a result of the curse of the law.

When man was under the curse of the law and we committed sin the best we could do is hope that GOD would have mercy on us. Now that we have peace with GOD under the New Covenant HE has given us the grace or HIS power to help us overcome the sin in our mortal bodies and overcome the sin of the world. So now let's study the last key that unlocks the door to your New Covenant rights and benefits which is:

Righteousness

In order for men to be righteous or in right standing with GOD they must free themselves from the law of sin and death by walking in the Spirit of Life by Christ Jesus. So, the first step to righteousness is making the confession of salvation. The second step is going through and completing the Romans 12:1-2 process designed to release your body from the lust and sin of the flesh and to renew your mind from the carnality of the world. John 8:32 clearly says: the truth shall MAKE you free but it is always quoted as: set you free. Roman's 10:9-10 sets you free from the world but you could backslide or fall back into captivity and sin. However, Romans 12:1-2 makes you free because that process transforms your soul from the desire for sin. Once you are made free sin is something you will no longer have a lust or desire to return to. After you have put-on Christ and have the Holy Spirit residing in you, Jesus can take up residence in you also and you will become a walking tabernacle or house of GOD. That is when you enter into righteousness with GOD and obtain the 4ᵗʰ key to the door of the New Covenant.

Romans

Chapter 8 verses 1-6 says

There is therefore now no condemnation to them which are in Christ Jesus, who walk not after the flesh, but after the Spirit.

² For the law of the Spirit of life [or New Covenant] in Christ Jesus has made me free from the law of sin and death.

³ For what the law could not do, in that it was weak through the flesh, GOD sending HIS own Son in the likeness of sinful flesh, and for sin, condemned sin in the flesh:

⁴ That the righteousness of the law might be fulfilled in us, who walk not after the flesh, but after the Spirit.

⁵ For they that are after the flesh do mind the things of the flesh; but they that are after the Spirit the things of the Spirit.

⁶ For to be carnally minded is death; but to be spiritually minded is life and peace.

And Romans Chapter 12:1-2 says:

I beseech you therefore, brethren, by the mercies of GOD, that you present your bodies a living sacrifice, holy, acceptable unto GOD, which is your reasonable service.

² And be not conformed to this world: but be you transformed by the renewing of your mind that you may prove what is that good, and acceptable, and perfect, will of GOD.

The good, acceptable, and perfect will of GOD is for you to be wealthy and live prosperously in peace. Once you renew your mind to think the way GOD designed you to think it will be easy then to be who the word of GOD says you are and do what the word of GOD says you can do.

If you want the word of GOD to produce a 100 fold return for you, you must come into righteousness and conform to the word and the will of GOD for your life. It has to be the true word of GOD not that which has been twisted, manipulated, and interpreted by religion. We can't just make the word of GOD say what we want it to say via religious doctrine and expect it to work the way we want it. According to Isaiah 55:11, the word of GOD will only work the way GOD intended. Therefore, we must have a firm grasp on what GOD actually meant when HE said what HE said and why HE said it through understanding. You see, knowledge is to know what GOD said and that's good. Wisdom is diligently doing what you know GOD said to do and that's acceptable. And understanding is to know why GOD said to do what HE said to do and that's perfect. Understanding gives you the ability to produce 100 fold. This is why GOD said in Proverbs 4:7 wisdom is the principle thing but in all your getting get understanding.

CHAPTER 4

NEW COVENANT IDENTITY, ABILITY AND POWER

"But you shall remember the Lord your GOD: for it is HE that gives you power to get wealth, that he may establish HIS covenant which HE swore unto your fathers, as it is this day (Deuteronomy 8:18)."

Once you are eligible to access the New Covenant, and you understand how to utilize the keys to enter into it, you must become qualified to enter and access all of its rights and benefits. The way you become qualified to receive the rights and benefits of the New Covenant is you must become transformed by the renewing of your mind so that you can come to the knowledge and complete understanding of who you are, what you have, and what you can do in Christ.

Religious leaders have kept you from being transformed into the person that GOD intended you to grow into suppressed by teaching you that it is crucial for you to be humble. Well, GOD said in Hebrews 4:16 come BOLDLY to the throne of grace that you might find grace or the power of GOD to help in the time of need. HE didn't say to come humbly. Nelson Mandela, one of history's greatest leaders, said: "You are a child of GOD. Your playing small does not serve the world." Yet, the contemporary leaders of religion teach you to make yourself small and to go before GOD begging when GOD said to come boldly.

The way religious leaders teach you to be humble is similar to the way domestic abusers expect their victims to be lowly in their presence. The word humble in this context means to destroy ones power, independence, and prestige. It is a form of the word "humiliate" where you allow someone to humble or abuse you mentally, emotionally, and spiritually. Humility damages your self respect and leads you to believe something is wrong with you since GOD does not appear to love you the same way HE does other people. Your relatives see this and wonder why you keep going back to that church like a domestic abuse victim keeps going back to their abuser.

The way religious leaders trick you into humiliating yourself is by twisting scriptures like Romans 12:3 where the Apostle Paul says: "For I say, through the grace given unto me, to every man that is among you, not to think *of himself* more highly than he ought to think; but to think soberly, according as GOD has dealt to every man the measure of faith." If you are reading from the King James Version you will notice that the words "of himself" are italicized which means those are words the translator added. The original translation should have read: for I say, through the grace given unto me, to every man that is among you, not to think more highly than he ought to think. The word "highly" was translated from the Greek word "hyperypsoo" which means to exalt yourself above others. Now, if you read that in context from verse 2-21 you will see what Paul was teaching is: after you have been transformed, renewed your mind, and have proven what is that good, acceptable, and perfect will of GOD don't be looking down your nose at some other person who hasn't competed their transformation yet.

You can think highly of yourself just don't look down your nose or hike up your tail because you think you are better than someone else. Here's the truth. The higher a monkey climbs the more he shows his butt. The altitude you reach in life will be determined by your attitude towards others. You see, the altitude of an airplane is affected by the relationship between its nose and its tail. When the plane's nose is turned down and its tail is hiked up it begins to fall. However, when the plane keeps its head or nose up and its tail down it will rise. If you don't act like a monkey when you are climbing to a new level in Christ Jesus, nobody will accuse you of showing your... butt.

Hosea 4:6 says: my people are destroyed for a lack of knowledge. It doesn't say my people are destroyed by haters, devils, or demons. You can be destroyed when you don't know what you are supposed to know such as who you are, what you have, and what you can do in Christ Jesus. When you don't know that false humility is a trick to keep you from being powerful you will always be pitiful. So, it is time to break out of the false humility of religious ideology to discover who you are, what you have, and what you can do under the New Covenant.

Who Are You In Christ Jesus?

You were not born in a vacuum without passion or purpose. You were created by GOD to be HIS son or daughter. As a child of GOD you are entitled to an inheritance because you are an heir to HIS kingdom. As an heir to the riches of the kingdom of GOD you should not be struggling financially! Prince William of England is entitled to an inheritance. Thus, he lives like a prince and gets treated like royalty simply because he is an heir of the queen.

However, you are an heir of the King of Kings. You are supposed to be wealthy and treated like royalty! Just as Prince William is treated as the queen is treated, you are entitled to be treated as GOD is treated! Now, religious people will try to make you believe that is blasphemy or sacrilege but look at what GOD said: "I said you are gods, and all of you are children of the most high (Psalm 82:6)." And "If my people who are called by my name... (2 Chronicles 7:14)"

You see, not only does GOD say that you are gods, HE also expects you to be called by HIS name. Every good father wants his kids to have his name. A man named Smith wants all of his children to be called Smith too. The Most High Father is no different. HIS name is GOD that is why HE said: "I said you are gods..." We carry the

NEW COVENANT IDENTITY, ABILITY AND POWER

family name or the name of our Father. Romans 8:16 says "The Holy Spirit bears witness that we are the children of GOD."

Next, the Apostle Paul said in Philippians 2:5-6 "Let this mind be in you which was also in Christ Jesus who being in the form of GOD thought it not robbery to be equal with GOD!" Again, the religious people will get mad and say that thinking you can be equal with GOD is blasphemy. However, you were made in the image & likeness of GOD. GOD made you as HE is or to be equal to HIM!

The religious leaders attacked Jesus because He called Himself the Son of GOD. In John 10:34 Jesus said "Is it not written in your law, I said, you are gods? So, why do you say that I'm blaspheming because I said I am the Son of GOD? The reason the religious leaders were upset is because under Jewish law once boys reach a certain age they become equal with their father. John 5:18 says the Jews sought to kill Jesus because He said GOD was His Father thus making himself equal with GOD. Jesus was beyond the age that a boy would be made equal with His Father therefore the Jews were upset. However, Jesus is equal with GOD and He prayed in John 17 that you would be equal with Him too.

Now, not only does GOD expect you to recognize that you are HIS child, HE also expects you to think and behave like HIS Son. HIS Son thought it not robbery to be equal With GOD therefore you are not to think it robbery to be equal with your Father.

So far, we have heard all three persons of the Triune Godhead: GOD, Jesus and the Holy Spirit, along with the Apostle Paul bearing witness that we are the children of GOD. Religious leaders who have a problem with you recognizing that you are a child of GOD simply want to keep you feeling ostracized and unworthy of being royalty. Romans 8:17 says that if we are in Christ then we are joint heirs with Jesus. That means you are not just a child of GOD but you are also an heir to the Kingdom of GOD!

Now that you know who you are in Christ Jesus lets discover what you have under the New Covenant. You have many things, a total of 58 blessings, but we will only cover 7 of them.

What You Have

First, as joint heirs with Jesus you are you entitled to receive an inheritance of abundance from the Kingdom of GOD. Therefore, you have the keys according to Matthew 6:19 to unlock or open the treasury room of heaven. You have access to the riches of the Kingdom of GOD so you have no reason to be struggling financially!

Secondly, Mark 4:11-12 says: unto **you** it is given to know the mystery of the Kingdom of GOD but unto them that are without, all these things are done in parables: that seeing they may see, and not perceive; and hearing they may hear, and not understand. You see, GOD provides sustenance to every person on earth but HE does not allow those who are not heir access to abundance. He keeps the mystery of what the Kingdom of GOD is and how to gain access to it a mystery for them. However, you are a child of GOD therefore that knowledge is being openly revealed to you. Even if they heard me saying this to you they don't have ears to hear. The eyes of their understanding have not been enlightened by the Holy Spirit so they won't get it.

Thirdly, you also have the right to expect to be treated like royalty because you are a royal heir. You have a right to expect to be treated as GOD is treated. Religious people may cry that is blaspheme but this is exactly why most religious people are poor! They love to wallow in false humility. They believe that GOD is a cruel master who will strike them down if they don't act humbly or pretend to believe they are less than what or who they really are. But this false humility is the very reason they remain in poverty.

In 2 Samuel chapter 9, there was a young man named Mephibosheth who was the grandson of King Saul and the son of Jonathan King David's best friend. David promised Jonathan before he died that he would take care of his children. So he asked a former servant of King Saul to find out if any of them were still alive. He told David about Mephibosheth who had been hidding in a city called Lodebar. His nurse thought that as the new king, David would kill off all the heirs of Saul or his relatives. So, in her haste to flee with the boy to save his life she fell on him and made him permanently lame in his feet.

Now when Mephibosheth came before David he fell on his face in reverence. This was an act of false humility because he had been told all of his life that David was going to kill him. But David said to him fear not: for I will surely show you kindness for Jonathan your father's sake, and will restore to you **all** the land of Saul your father; and you shall eat bread at my table continually. In response to David's promise Mephibosheth bowed himself (still being fearful and religious) and said, what is your servant that you should look upon **such a dead dog as I am?** Then David said: I have given you all that pertained to Saul and to all his house and you shall eat at my table as one of the king's sons.

You see, fear and false religious reverence kept Mephibosheth living in a city called Lodebar which means a place of poverty. Fear and belief in false religious traditions that grow out of living in a community with a poverty mentality kept him from accepting his rightful place of royalty and kept him out of position to receive his inheritance. Fear led him to genuflect in a false humility and act as if he was unworthy to stand before the king. Fear, false beliefs, and bad teaching made him not only lame of feet but also lame of heart. False humility is offensive to GOD because it makes HIS sons that HE created to be powerful appear to be pitiful. Bad teaching, false doctrine, and religious tradition have made the men of GOD lame of feet: unworthy to stand before GOD. It has also made them lame of heart because they don't feel strong enough to walk with GOD as Adam did in the Garden.

Under the New Covenant you have the right to stand before GOD as HIS heir and to walk with GOD as HIS son or daughter. You have the right to eat continually at HIS table which has been prepared before your enemies so they can see you being blessed. Now, GOD is not going to violate your will so you have the choice to live on the abundance level or you can live on GOD's Aid for Dependent Children, Section 8, food stamp or SNAP level of subsistence like religious people do. I don't know about you, but as for me and my house, we will be SERVED WITH the Lord!

The fourth thing you have in Christ under the New Covenant is GOD's Word. You have the logos or written word and you are entitled to receive the rhema or inspired word once you learn how to diligently study. And you have the power contained in the logos word as well as the authority to utilize that power. The word will work, if you work it!

The fifth thing you have under the New Covenant is GOD's Will. GOD has a twofold will: perfect and permissive or boulema and thelema in the Greek language respectively. GOD's perfect, or boulema, will is what HE intended everything to be from creation. GOD's permissive or thelema will is what HE allows you to do because of the sovereignty HE has given you to rule and reign in the earth. GOD's perfect will for you is to live like royalty. But HE will allow you, by HIS permissive will, to be lowly and live in abject poverty if you want to.

The sixth blessing that you are entitled to receive under the New Covenant is the Holy Spirit. According to Acts 1:8, the Holy Spirit gives you power to be a witness to the preeminent existence of the True and Living GOD and that both HE and HIS power reside in us.

The seventh blessing you have under the New Covenant is Jesus, Son of the Living GOD, who is the only deity among the more than 140,000 religions world-wide **BOLD** enough to declare: "**I** am the way the truth, and the life. No man comes unto the Father but by **Me**!" In Him you have **all** things that pertain to life and godliness.

Now that you know who you are and what you have under the New Covenant let's talk about:

What You Can Do In Christ Jesus

Philippians 4:13 says you can do all things through Christ who strengthens you.

Colossians 1:27 says with Christ in you it gives you the ability to achieve the hope of GOD's glory for your life.

The word "Christ" has three different Greek meanings that essentially describe the power we receive from being in Christ to perform various acts which is called the anointing. The anointing is the power that GOD lends natural men to enable them to do supernatural things. The anointing is different from the grace (or power of GOD) that GOD equips men with to take dominion and authority over the earth. The anointing is the power that makes all things that appear to be impossible possible. The anointing is the power part of faith that Jesus lent to all those people whom He told: your faith has made you whole. Therefore, you can do all things through the anointing or the power of GOD which strengthens you.

Now, the word "glory" is being used in Colossians 1:27 in a manner that indicates a job, mission, or purpose has been completed or fulfilled. We give a loved one, for example, a day of glory after they have graduated high school or college. The Greek word for this is "kauchaomai" which means to exalt, celebrate, or rejoice in the context of the completion or fulfillment of an assignment or mission like the parades cities host for pro teams that win a championship. Thus, the word glory should be translated to either completion or fulfillment in this verse and read as follows:

To whom GOD would make known what is the riches of the fulfillment of this mystery among the Gentiles; which is the anointing or the power of GOD in you, the hope of completion. That is, the hope that GOD has of you completing the mission or assignment that HE has given you the anointing or HIS power to fulfill.

There is a reason GOD placed you here. There is a purpose that GOD wants you to complete or fulfill that will benefit mankind before you exit this planet. That job or assignment is unique to the knowledge, gifts, talents, and abilities that HE placed in you when you were born. It is a job that nobody can do but you.

Therefore, whenever GOD speaks to you it will be pertaining to something that HE wants you to do. With GOD everything is always about going and doing. This is why one of the pieces of armor in the whole armor of GOD is foot wear or having your feet shod with the preparation of the gospel of peace. If you analyze the name of GOD you will notice that two thirds of HIS name spelled forward is GO and two thirds of HIS name spelled backward is DO. When GOD gives you a command to GO and DO that is a GOD Ordained Divine Opportunity to achieve glory. All of the heroes in the Hebrews 11 hall of fame of faith obtained glory because GOD said go and do, and by faith they went and did.

Now, we have five voices that we have to contend with on a daily basis that are ALL trying to control what we go and do. Those voices are: the voice of our spirit, the voice of our mind, the voice of our body (when you want a cookie that is your body speaking), the voice of GOD, and the voice of the devil who always tries to pretend that he is GOD. Therefore, we must know how to tell the difference between all the other voices and the voice of GOD.

The voice of GOD when heard outside of us is thunderous, sounds like rushing rivers, and is powerful. When you get a chance read: John 12:28-29, Ezekiel 43:2, and Psalms 29:4 and you will see what I mean. GOD's voice will always be in concert and never in conflict with HIS word. The devil's voice is always deceiving, tempting, and tormenting. Read Matthew 4, Genesis 3, and Mark Chapters 5 and 9. There you will see that the devil will always try to use the word in an effort to make us believe that he is GOD speaking but his word will always be a twisted version of GOD's word.

Now, when GOD speaks to us from the inside it comes up in a still or quiet manner that sounds like a harmonious or melodic tone. Until our body is made a living sacrifice unto GOD whenever we hear the voice of GOD our inclination is to go in the opposite direction; to run and hide. This is the reason after something bad happened you said: something told me to or something told me not to. That something was the voice of GOD trying to guide, direct, and protect you but you chose to do the opposite of what HE said to do.

Our instinct to go in the opposite direction is the reason I believe GOD chooses to speak to us quietly and melodically. This reminds me of a teacher I had in high school. Whenever he tried to give us personal advice and we didn't agree he would respond in a quiet musical tone: by saying: allllriiiight sucka! At the end of the day we would find out that he was right and would have to do what he said anyway. I believe, therefore, that GOD speaks using harmony or the musical scale to lead us into harmony or in agreement with HIS will as well as to teach us a lesson.

NEW COVENANT IDENTITY, ABILITY AND POWER

The musical scale is: do, re, me, fa, so, la, ti, do. Now, the first note is pronounced doe but it is actually do because with GOD everything HE says is an instruction to go and do. Since we tend to run in an opposite direction from what GOD said to do we usually find our self in difficulty and eventually have to go back to the point where we disobeyed GOD when HE told us to "do".

We end up going back up the musical scale to the beginning but only after reaching the end of the scale and realizing we ran into the same instruction: do! We never realized that at the beginning and the end of the music scale you will find the same command for GOD: "do". This is teaching you that you can run and hide but at the end of the day you will always have to "do" what GOD said. There is power, riches, and glory or fulfillment waiting for us if we would just do whatever GOD gave us an assignment to complete or fulfill.

Colossians 1:18-19 says: "And He [Jesus] is the head of the body, the church: who is the beginning, the firstborn from the dead; that in **all** things He might have the preeminence (which translated from the Greek word "proteuo" means first or first example). For it pleased the Father that in Him should all fullness dwell (Colossians 1:18-19)."

You see, GOD made Jesus after HIS likeness to provide us with an example of what HE wanted us to be like. Then GOD sent Jesus here to do various exploits to be an example of what HE expects us to do. That means, whatever we have seen Jesus do in the word it was put there as an example to show us what we can do in the world.

What we can do in Christ is utilize His power to cast out demons, heal the sick, and mend the broken hearted. We can control our environment, just as Jesus controlled the wind and the waves of the sea, just as Jesus walked on the water and Peter followed after, we can do this and more if we only have the faith to believe that we can.

Psalms 121:1-2 says: "I will lift up my eyes unto the hills from whence comes my help. My help comes from the LORD."

As a child of GOD you cannot enjoy the full rights and benefits of the New Covenant until you go through the Romans 12:1-2 process and become an adult in Christ Jesus. GOD has given you an opportunity to receive your rights and benefits through the system of the Kingdom of GOD. Now, you have to go in and possess them. As GOD told the children of Israel, I have given you the Promised Land now you have to take possession of it. The devil and his disciples have found a way to wall you away from your rightful possessions to keep you from taking them. This is why Jesus said: the Kingdom of GOD suffers violence and the violent take it by force. GOD will show you how to fight the devil and win, like HE did with Joshua at the battle of Jericho. But GOD's way is not our way so HE is going to tell you something to do that is weird to you but if you just do what HE says that wall will fall flat for you too.

"So the people shouted when the priests blew with the trumpets: and it came to pass, when the people heard the sound of the trumpet, and the people shouted with a great shout, that the wall fell down flat, so that the people went up into the city, every man straight before him, and they took the city (Joshua 6:20)."

Most people didn't know that the walls of Jericho were wide enough for houses to sit on top and for chariots to ride back and forth on a two-lane street. Rahab the harlot's house was on top of the wall. This is why she was able to let Joshua's spies down the wall through her back window to escape without being seen. This tells you the phrase "fell flat" does not mean the walls fell over on their side because they would still be too high for every man to simply walk straight before him to take the city. Instead of walking straight ahead they would have had to climb up about 20 yards of wall. The phrase fell flat is how a building falls that is taken down by controlled demolition. It collapses flat on its own footprint. When the walls of Jericho came down they simply dropped straight down below the ground. You can go there today and see them submerged below the dirt.

The devil and his disciples have the wealth that GOD laid up for you walled off. Therefore, you will have to go in and take possession of it. If you do what GOD tells you to do, HE will make that wall collapse for you and then you can walk straight in and take it by force.

CHAPTER 5

TRAPPED IN CAPTIVITY

"In the third year of the reign of Jehoiakim king of Judah came Nebuchadnezzar king of Babylon unto Jerusalem and besieged it (Daniel 1:1)."

When you study the Old Testament and watch the growth and development of the children of Israel you will notice a cycle where they constantly vacillated in and out of sin. They would have a period where they followed the True and Living GOD faithfully but over time they would fall back into Babylonian captivity as a result of worshiping idol or pagan gods. Once the people stopped paying attention to how they were worshiping the Most High GOD the spirit of Babylon would always creep back in and they'd start worshiping pagan and idol gods again. GOD would have to afflict them for their actions by letting them go into captivity each time. Read 2 Kings 9:16 through 10:28 and you will see GOD sent Jehu to bring judgment upon King Ahab, Queen Jezebel, and their whole family for leading the children of Israel to worship the Babylonian god Baal. The children of Israel would repent, worship GOD faithfully for a while, then the spirit of Babylon would creep back in, and the cycle would start all over again. In Revelation 2:13-16 Jesus says to the church:

"I know your works and where you dwell, even where Satan's seat is: and you hold fast my name, and have not denied my faith... but I have a few things against you because you have them there that hold the doctrine of Balaam, who taught Balac to cast a stumbling-block before the children of Israel, to eat things sacrificed unto idols, and to commit fornication. So have you also them that hold the doctrine of the Nicolaitanes which thing I hate. Repent or else I will come unto you quickly and will fight against them with the sword of my mouth (Revelation 2:13-16)."

We are currently living in a cycle where the the church and the people of GOD are being afflicted with debt, poverty, and many medical maladies because the spirit of Babylon has crept back into the church as evidenced by the presence of the doctrine of the Nicolatianes. That is the doctrine that leads the people of GOD to worship their preachers and inadvertently make him/her an idol god. The name "Nicolaitans" comes from the Greek word nikolaos which means one who conquers and subdues the people. The doctrine of the Nicolaitans is where the term "spiritual father" comes from that subtly leads GOD's people to make the preacher their lord instead of Jesus.

Therefore, GOD's people are struggling spiritually and financially because when a preacher promises you that GOD is "about to" or "getting ready to" bless you GOD makes them responsible for fulfilling that promise. Your preacher is in the business of taking not giving. Greed is where you enter into a relationship with the intent to get more than you give. Preachers teach you to be greedy by leading you to believe you only need to give a little to GOD in order to get a lot. Greed is one of the seven deadly sins. This is one reason why the breakthrough that your preacher promises GOD is about to do for you never breaks through.

The church going people of GOD are unwittingly worshiping a pagan god under the spirit of Babylon while under the fervent belief that they are worshiping the True and Living GOD. At the same time, they have heard of the blessings of GOD's abundance under the New Covenant but they cannot figure out why they have not received that blessing. They go to church faithfully, tithe, give, and volunteer however nothing is working. They catch glimpses of GOD's blessings here and there but they have not been blessed with the abundance promised under the New Covenant. GOD said: my people are destroyed for a lack of knowledge. GOD's people are being slowly destroyed because they don't know that they have been worshiping under the spirit of Babylon which has walled them off from their rights and benefits of the New Covenant. In order to receive the abundance they want the people of GOD must repent, cast out the spirit of Babylon from their lives, and prepare to enter the New Covenant promise.

You can enter the promise of the New Covenant and become eligible to receive an inheritance through the Romans 10:9-10 confession of salvation. However, being eligible to receive an inheritance does not mean you are qualified to get it. The full rights and benefits of the New Covenant belong to those who have given GOD life service not just lip service. Matthew 6:33 reveals two of the qualifiers: seek you first the kingdom of GOD and secondly you must seek GOD's righteousness not your righteousness, your preacher's, or your religion's standard of righteousness. Ergo, you cannot access the benefits of the New Covenant until you come into righteousness or in right standing with GOD by completing the Romans 12:1-2 transformation process.

It will be difficult to complete the transformation process if you go to a church where they teach you to be greedy while feeding you the milk of the word excessively rather than strong meat. When adults drink too much milk it produces mucus that depresses your spiritual immune system. Milk is a Babylonian stumbling-block that makes adults spiritually sick, weak, and easy to defeat. Some Christian adult daycare centers that pose as churches serve flavored milk. The sugar in flavored milk makes people feel energized so they believe they are being fed something different but it's still milk not meat. Those who want to make the transformation to enter into GOD's righteousness must be willing to give up the Babylonian milk of the word and become ready to receive strong meat.

"…we have many things to say and hard to be uttered, seeing you are dull of hearing [or understanding]; for when for the time you ought to be teachers, you have need that one teach you again which be the first principles of the oracles of GOD; and are become such as have need of milk, and not of strong meat. For every one that uses milk is unskillful in the word of righteousness: for he is a babe. But strong meat belongs to them that are of full age, even those who by reason of use have their senses exercised to discern both good and evil. Therefore leaving the principles of the doctrine of Christ, let us go on unto perfection; not laying again the foundation of repentance from dead works, of faith toward GOD, of the doctrine of baptisms, of laying on of hands, of resurrection of the dead, and of eternal judgment (Hebrews 5:11-6:2)."

The average Christian who goes to church every week cannot figure out why, after all their diligent church attendance, volunteer service, and tithing they are still struggling to enter into GOD's promise of abundance. The reason they cannot enter into abundance because they have not yet entered into righteousness. They have come out of the world into church but they still have the world in them. They have gotten saved but they have yet to be converted and transformed by completing the Romans 12:1-2 process. They don't realize that the blood running through their veins is not the blood of Jesus. Their blood is still contaminated by the lusts of the world and the Babylonian doctrines and traditions of religion which are anti-GOD and anti-

Christ. They proclaim Christ as their savior but they have not put on Christ so they are not in Christ.

"And you shall know the truth, and the truth shall **make** you free (John 8:32)."

"…if you shall confess with your mouth the Lord Jesus, and shall believe in your heart that GOD has raised Him from the dead, you shall be saved. For with the heart man believes unto righteousness; and with the mouth confession is made unto salvation (Romans 10:9-10)."

"I beseech you therefore, brethren, by the mercies of GOD, that you present your bodies a living sacrifice, holy, acceptable unto GOD, which is your reasonable service. And be not conformed to this world: but be you transformed by the renewing of your mind, that you may prove what is that good, and acceptable, and perfect will of GOD (Romans 12:1-2)."

John 8:32 clearly says the truth shall MAKE you free yet everyone you know, including your favorite preacher, quotes that verse as: the truth shall SET you free. This is important because there is a critical difference between the words: make and set. When you are set free you can either choose to go back and backslide or you can be taken back into captivity. When you are made free you are free indeed. You cannot be taken back into captivity legally when you are made free and you lose all lust, nostalgia and desire to return voluntarily because you are free indeed or in all that you desire to do.

Making the confession described in Romans 10:9-10 will set you free from the captivity of sin and death in the world and make you eligible to enter heaven. However, you could backslide and return to the world and into sin voluntarily. Therefore, you must be made free by being converted into Christ Jesus and transformed into Christ likeness as one of GOD's daughters or sons through the renewing of your mind. Once you have proven that you have sacrificed your body to reject sin and are walking in the good, acceptable and perfect will of GOD, or in HIS righteousness, HE will give you your inheritance of access to the riches of the Kingdom of GOD.

Access to the New Covenant riches in the Kingdom of GOD is the New Testament Promised Land. Although the people of GOD go to church every week they are still circling the wilderness because very few of them have actually completed the Romans 12:1-2 transformation process. Once the Hebrews got out of Egypt GOD would not allow them to enter the Promised Land until they got the Egypt out of them. They came out of Egypt trying to hold on to the religious doctrine and tradition their captors had given them and were still trying to worship Babylonian gods. The people of GOD today have the same problem. They are bound in captivity to religious doctrine and tradition and are still worshiping Babylonian gods unwittingly.

Additionally, church going people of GOD are still stuck on the cross. They are stuck there because that is where they have stuck Jesus by continuing to follow Old Covenant law. As a result they have made His sacrifice to initiate the New Covenant grace of none effect in their lives. Romans 4:14 says: "For if they which are of the law be heirs, faith is made void, and the promise made of none effect." The consequence of keeping Jesus stuck on the cross is a lack of movement in their Christian development into GOD's righteousness. They are stuck at the vortex of the cross never moving left or right and never going up or down. So they are stuck in the same place they have always been with no access to their New Covenant rights and benefits. Until GOD's people break out of religion, come down off the cross, and let Jesus ascend into His Kingdom they will always be stuck living in subsistence rather than abundance.

Finally, I want to send a message to preachers who teach in a way that leads church going people to be stuck in subsistence rather than living in abundance. GOD's people love to quote John 3:16 to introduce people of the world to the love of GOD but unfortunately they stop at verse 16. Therefore, they don't understand that verse 16 is a preamble to GOD's warning to preachers who are in darkness to come back to the light. John 3:16 is NOT an exhortation to people of the world. It is a warning the people of GOD also who are following their preachers into darkness to come back to the light as well. Jesus said in Matthew 15:14 that when the blind leads the blind they will all fall into a ditch. The word "ditch" is a reference to the pit of hell. I don't want you to end up in hell for following a preacher who you thought was doing the right thing. I also want to relieve you of your spiritual blindness to help you see who you are following and where you are going clearly, so let's study John 3:16-21 closely.

"...GOD so loved the world, that HE gave HIS only begotten Son, that whosoever believeth in Him should not perish, but have everlasting life. For GOD sent not HIS Son into the world to condemn the world; but that the world through Him might be saved.

He that believes on Him is not condemned: but he that believes **not** is condemned already, because he has not believed in the name of the only begotten Son of GOD. And this is the condemnation...

[GOD is saying, OK, this is the reason why church people at the advent of the New Testament were condemned and this is the same reason many people in the church are being condemned today.]

...that light [or because Jesus who is the light of the world] is come into the world, and men loved darkness rather than light, because their deeds were evil.

[GOD is saying that HE sent Jesus to be a light for men of GOD but they rejected the light because the truth of the light would reveal that their deeds were evil.]

For every one that does evil hates the light neither comes to the light, lest his deeds should be reproved. But he that does truth comes to the light, that his deeds may be made manifest, that they are wrought in GOD [or to prove that they are the work of GOD] (John 3:16-21)."

Jesus is saying plainly, if you keep following preachers who are roaming around in darkness that refuse to come to the light of truth because they would rather twist truth into a lie so they can con you out of your money, you will be condemned right along with them. You must know that when preachers refuse to walk in the light of truth due to their heart for deceit and lust for sex and money GOD gives them over to their vile affections. Therein they begin to do all manner of evil to, with, and among their selves. GOD is warning you that if you continue to follow them, you will be infected by the evil spirit that is operating in their heart, so GOD will have to give you over to vile affections too. Let's look at Romans 1:18-26.

"...the wrath of GOD is revealed from heaven against all ungodliness and unrighteousness of men, who hold the truth in unrighteousness. [GOD is saying HIS wrath is falling on preachers hold the truth yet they choose to be unrighteous; now how does GOD know they hold the truth: verse 19]

Because that which **may** be known of GOD is manifest **in** them; for GOD has **showed** it to them [GOD is saying here: I know they know the truth because I showed it to them; verse 20].

For the invisible things of HIM [meaning GOD] from the creation of the world are clearly seen, being understood by the things that are made, even HIS eternal power and GODHEAD; so that they are without excuse [GOD said, I've showing them hidden mysteries about the creation of the world and how I used the power of the triune GODHEAD to make everything that was made so they cannot use the excuse: I didn't know; verse 21]:

Because that, when they **knew** GOD, they glorified HIM not as GOD, neither were thankful; but became vain in their imaginations, and their foolish heart was darkened [GOD is teaching us a lesson on how familiarity breeds contempt. HE said, because they knew or had intimate knowledge of me as GOD they did not glorify me as GOD and began to imagine in their hearts that they could be god. So HE turned off the light that they had access to and their hearts became darkened; verses 22 & 23].

Professing themselves to be wise, they became fools, and changed the glory of the incorruptible GOD into an image made like to corruptible man, and to birds, and four footed beasts, and creeping things [you see, once men grow to have contempt for the Most High GOD they create images of gods in their hearts spiritually, and idols to represent physically what they believe GOD should be; verse 24-26].

Wherefore [or this is another reason] GOD also gave them up to uncleanness through the lusts of their own hearts, to dishonor their own bodies between themselves: who changed the **truth** of GOD into a lie, and worshipped and served the creature more than the Creator, who is blessed forever; for this cause GOD gave them up to vile affections... (Romans 1:18-26)"

If you are that person who "loves" your preacher to the point where you believe he could do no wrong, you may be one who believe that by serving your preacher you are serving GOD. You could be one who is unwittingly serving the creature more than the Creator. You could actually be worshipping your preacher while believing you are worshiping GOD. Now, watch how preachers in darkness, that change the truth of GOD into a lie, react when they hear me reveal this truth. They don't want to you come to the truth so they won't be exposed by the light. Therefore, they will try to make you believe that I'm not telling the truth using the devil's tactic of raising questions about the truth teller: who is this guy, where did he come from, what church does he go to, where did he go to school, and so on. Since the truth is incontrovertible they have to make you question the veracity of the truth teller by suggesting: if you don't know the truth about him, how can you know he is telling the truth about this? Their last ditch effort is to make up lies about the truth teller, as they did with Jesus, to make you condemn him.

However, if you are not one who blindly follows the devil's disciples, you can see with your own eyes proof that GOD has given them up to vile affection in today's headlines. You've seen scandal after scandal where preachers are accused of molesting children and raping girls. You see preachers working everyday to and lead women into church under the pretext of praying with them when they intend to prey on them financially because they have a vile affection for money. You see reports about women that were seduced by preachers who have a vile affection for exerting power and control through sexual activity. You see them leading you to remain in their captivity by teaching you that you are not supposed to judge so that you won't judge them after you discover the truth about them. However, the Apostle Paul said in 1 Corinthians 6:2-3:

"Do you not know that the saints shall judge the world; and if the world shall be judged by you, are you unworthy to judge the smallest matters? Know you not that **we** shall judge angels; how much more things that pertain to this life?"

The Apostle Paul is teaching us, contrary to popular belief, that GOD has ordained HIS people to judge the world. Your preacher teaches you to judge not lest you be judged because he needed to misquote Matthew 7:1 to protect his self from being judged by his church members if he got caught in a scandal. But Paul says your job is to judge the world so why do you think that you are unworthy to judge a small matter like the sins of your preacher? The reason you believe that you are unworthy to judge is because your preacher set you up to rest in that conclusion by twisting Romans 3:23 that says: for all have sinned, and come short of the glory of GOD.

You see, the preachers of darkness want you to conclude that you cannot judge them if you are a sinner too. That verse, however is talking about people who choose to walk in the law rather than the glory of GOD's grace. Sin is simply refusing to do what GOD wants you to do and instead choosing to do what you want to do. Ergo, all who don't do what GOD wants them to do have sinned. Preachers of darkness who sin by refusing to walk in the light of GOD fall short of GOD's glory (or finishing the work HE sent them to complete) therefore HE gives them up to vile affections to be consumed by their own lust. The people of GOD who want to receive their full rights and benefits under the New Covenant must turn away from those preachers who lead you to lust for houses, cars, clothes, money, and things and turn toward those you can teach you how to receive abundant living through the system of the kingdom of GOD.

CHAPTER 6

DEFINING TRUE WORSHIP

"GOD is a Spirit and they that worship HIM must worship HIM in spirit and in truth (John 4:24)."

This is sad to say, but it's too late for church going people over age 70 who would rather die than give up their old time religion to enter the New Covenant Promised Land. Like the Hebrew elders that came out of Egyptian captivity they refuse to let go of the doctrine and traditions of Babylonian religion. They have been going to church some 50, 60, or 70 years of their lives but they have never made the Romans 12:1-2 transformation to get the lusts and influences of Egypt out of them and actually enter into GOD's righteousness. Therefore, like Moses, they cannot enter into the New Covenant Promised Land and GOD has sentenced them to die in the wilderness. The younger generation on the other hand has an opportunity to enter GOD's new covenant and live in abundance. They just need a Joshua to lead them out of the Egyptian wilderness into the Promised Land. That is out of the Old Testament bondage of Egyptian mental captivity and Babylonian religious bondage and into the New Covenant grace where there is power, provision, protection, and peace.

One of the ways church going people get tricked into practicing Babylonian religion is they don't know GOD's definition of the words: worship, thanksgiving, and praise. No one ever taught them that giving "thanks" should not be confused with "thanksgiving" because the former is powerful and the latter is being respectful and grateful. Thanksgiving simply means to express gratitude to GOD for what HE has done. Understand, now, that we don't thank GOD for what HE will do because GOD is a now GOD. There is no time with GOD except the present. Jesus said in Mark 11:24 to believe you received at the time you prayed and you will have whatever you prayed for. If you don't believe you have already received the answer at the very moment you prayed, even though it has not yet manifested, you are not operating in faith because faith is now. Faith is now because GOD "is" not was or will be. Therefore, our thanksgiving goes up to GOD in all things and at all times because we know GOD has already given us whatever we could imagine to ask HIM for.

Giving thanks on the other hand has the same connotation and produces the same result as the word "blessed" which means: empower to prosper. Giving thanks empowers the person or the thing that we prayed over or for to prosper, be fruitful, or multiply exponentially. Since GOD gave us dominion and authority in the earth, we give thanks to give GOD permission to prosper us, make us fruitful, and multiply our supply exponentially. The prayer Jesus prayed when giving thanks is called the prayer of supplication. That is a prayer where we believe GOD to supplement what we already have or to exponentially multiply our supply.

"And He [Jesus] asked them: How many loaves have you? And they said seven... and He took the seven loaves, and gave thanks, and brake, and gave to his disciples to set before them... and they had a few small fishes: and He blessed and commanded to set them also before them. So they did eat... and they that had eaten were about four thousand (Mark 8:5-9)."

"One of His [Jesus'] disciples Andrew, Simon Peter's brother, said to Him: There is a lad here who has five barley loaves and two small fishes: but what are they among so many? And Jesus said: Make the men sit down... so the men sat down in number about five thousand. And Jesus took the loaves; and when He had given thanks He distributed to the disciples, and the disciples to them that were set down; and likewise of the fishes as much as they wanted (John 8:8-11)."

You see, each time Jesus gave thanks whatever He prayed over multiplied exponentially. The real reason we "bless" the food at our family table is not for protection from poison or to be superstitious. It's to agree with GOD that the food will be fruitful, prosperous, and increase so that everyone can eat until they are satisfied. The word "thanks" in this context comes from the Greek word "homologeo" which means to agree or to increase supply. Giving thanks activates the power GOD gave us to increase our supply exceedingly above whatever we could ask or think. The fervent effectual prayer of a righteous man availeth much or makes much available. The power to multiply exponentially through blessing or giving thanks is the reason the woman of Zerephath's barrel of meal and cruse of oil, in 1 Kings 17, never ran empty during 3 years of famine. This is the same power the Prophet Elisha used to cause a woman's jar of oil to flow until she ran out of pots to pour it into in 2 Kings 4. Hopefully that provided clarity on the difference between giving thanks and thanksgiving.

Now, praise is simply giving GOD immense and intense glory and honor for what HE has done through us to prosper our families and for what HE has given us the power to do in HIS name. Psalm 100:4 says: enter HIS gates with thanksgiving and enter HIS courts with praise. The word "gates" comes from the Hebrew word "sa'ar" which means: entrance to a city or the city of the Kingdom of GOD. And the word "courts" is translated from the Hebrew word "haser" which means: an enclosed or exclusive area. Praise serves like a type of voice recognition password that authorizes us to enter the kingdom of GOD or the treasury room of heaven and exercise our exclusive right to partake in the commonwealth of the children of GOD. If GOD has never heard you praise HIM in intimate sincerity and you try to enter the kingdom of GOD, HE will say depart from me you worker of iniquity I never knew you. Jesus said my sheep know my voice.

Conversely, if you are one of His true sheep, He recognizes your voice too.

"Wherefore remember that you being in time past Gentiles in the flesh... were without Christ being aliens from the commonwealth of Israel, and strangers from the covenants of promise... but now in Christ Jesus you... are made nigh by the blood of Christ (Ephesians 2:11-13)."

Now, as it pertains to worship our idea of what it is and how it is expressed must be taken out of the context of religion so we can acquire the proper understanding. In Ephesians 6:15 the Apostle Paul describes the armor of GOD that covers the feet. Take note here that he calls the foot covering: "the preparation of the gospel of peace." Why is the gospel compared to a type of footwear? It's because GOD expects you to take the gospel of peace or to take the word of GOD with you everywhere you go. The word worship is a compound word that is comprised of the words: word and ship. When GOD uses the word "worship" HE means: to take the word and go. It is similar to the word fellowship: friends or fellows going somewhere together. Worship simply means to put feet to our faith. This is confirmed by the Great Commission of Jesus in Matthew 28:19 where He said: Go therefore and teach all nations. How will you teach all nations? You will teach them with the truth of the word of GOD. And thereby baptize them with the water of the word in the name of the Father, and of the Son, and of the Holy Ghost.

We have the wrong definition of worship and the wrong idea of how to worship because the devil's disciples do everything they can through false doctrine to stop you from taking the word of GOD everywhere with you. They do everything they can to trick you out of obeying the Great Commission and teaching all nations with the truth. Evangelicals fight politically for prayer in school to mislead you into believing they are trying to execute the Great Commission. However, their false religiosity blinds them to the reality that there's no need to have prayer in school if you send your kids to school with prayer in them. We don't need to have an atheist or an unbelieving teacher forced to deliver the word in school if our kids go to school with the word in them. GOD gave us faith, the word, and prayer to make us powerful but religion and religious men distract us with political issues to make us powerless and to keep us in bondage.

"Nebuchadnezzar the king made an image of gold, whose height was threescore cubits, and the breadth thereof six cubits: he set it up in the plain of Dura, in the province of Babylon... to you it is commanded, O people... that at what time you hear the sound of the cornet, flute, harp, sackbut, psaltery, dulcimer, and all kinds of music, you fall down and worship the golden image that Nebuchadnezzar the king hath set up (Daniel 3:1-4b-5)."

When evangelicals go to the political arena to get politicians to make laws to force faith, the word, and prayer in the public space that is a Babylonian religious practice. Their works keep the people of

GOD in bondage because their actions are driven by the spirit of Babylon. Their works to demand laws that require people to worship in the public space is no different than king Nebuchadnezzar's law that required people to worship the image he set up. Evangelicals are in reality subtly preparing the people of GOD to worship the beast that will be set up by the anti-Christ. The reason so many people will worship the anti-Christ when he appears is because Evangelicals will point to him and say that he is Christ.

"And they worshipped the dragon which gave power unto the beast: and they worshipped the beast saying: who is like unto the beast? Who is able to make war with him (Revelation 13:4)?"

"...because of false brethren unawares brought in, who came in privately to spy out our liberty which we have in Christ Jesus, that they might bring us into bondage... knowing that a man is not justified by the works of the law, but by the faith of Jesus Christ, even we have believed in Jesus Christ, that we might be justified by the faith of Christ, and not by the works of the law: for by the works of the law shall no flesh be justified (Galatians 2:4, 16)."

As Christians we worship GOD because we love HIM and we want to keep HIS commandment or the Great Commission. Jesus said in John 14:15, if you love me keep my commandments. However, most of the acts we engage in as a form of worship are nothing more than works of the flesh designed to keep us in bondage to the law rather than to keep HIS commandments. The devil's disciples lead GOD's people to believe that performing these religious acts of worship will make you justified in the sight of GOD or keep you in righteousness with HIM. But, if you understand the Apostle Paul's treatise on works of the flesh you will see clearly the truth contradicts religion's false doctrine and tradition.

"...if Abraham was justified by works he has reason to glory; but not before GOD. For what says the scripture? Abraham believed GOD and it was counted unto him for righteousness. Now to him that work is the reward reckoned of debt not of grace. But to him that work not, but believe on Him that justifies the ungodly, his faith is counted for righteousness. Even as David also described the blessedness of the man unto whom GOD imputed righteousness without works (Romans 4:2-6)."

You see, worship as a religious act of trying to be righteous is offensive to GOD not endearing. Let's take a look at several of the Hebrew and Greek definitions of the word "worship" and we will see that the way we have been taught to worship through religious tradition has served to put us in enmity with GOD rather than in righteousness before HIM. The Hebrew words we will highlight are: gid, asab, and saba:

- **Gid** – pay honor

• **Asab** – to grieve, interfere with, be distressed, to shape, make an image of, displeased, sorry, hurt, filled with pain, vexed

• **Saba** – weigh down, cause to bow, made to bow, made obeisance, fall down, crouch, fell flat, made stoop, humbly beseech, reverence

Simply examining the Hebrew or Old Testament definitions of the word "worship" should alert us immediately that the way we worship actually grieves GOD. Now, when we examine the Greek words that translated into the English word "worship" which are: doxa, ethelothreskia, eusebeo, latreuo, proskyneo, and Sebo. These words more accurately reveal the traditional religious meanings of the word worship. When you don't understand the true meaning of words the devil can trick you into grieving GOD while making you believe that you are worshiping GOD.

• **Doxa** – glory or honor

• **Ethelothreskia** – self imposed religion, will worship

• **Eusebeo** – put religion into practice, piety show (you will see a Pharisee exercising this kind of worship in Luke 11:43-44 and 18:10-14 and you will know immediately why GOD doesn't like it)

• **Latreuo** – serve religious, duty, minister

- **Proskyneo** – pay homage, show reverence, kneel down (this may sound good if you don't know GOD said to come boldly to the throne of grace not like a lowly beggar)

- **Sebo** – to be devout, religious

Do you see that our traditional use of the word worship, by Greek definition, is associated with the practice of religion which is the devil's counterfeit form of relation. GOD wanted to have a relationship with HIS creation but the devil offered man religion to lead us out of relationship with GOD and took us into captivity. If you examine what Jesus was doing during His ministry objectively, He was trying to free us by tearing down the doctrines and traditions of religion. Jesus was trying to revolutionize our concept of worship to lead us to move from religion back into relation. GOD wants worship to be like a relationship where two people are "going together" in agreement with HIS word. GOD wants us to worship HIM through word ship or by taking the word into our heart, going somewhere with it, and allowing the Holy Spirit to help us deliver it.

CHAPTER 7

A NEW ATTITUDE

"Be you therefore perfect, even as your Father which is in heaven is perfect (Matthew 5:48)."

You need a new attitude about the word of GOD, religion, and wealth in order to fully benefit from the New Covenant. A new attitude will empower you to transform your mind and give you the capacity to think on a higher operant order. When you can think on a higher order it will increase your capacity and enable you to achieve and receive more. This is no different than placing an order for any commodity. The bigger or higher your order the more you receive. The more you have increases your opportunity to translate what you received into wealth.

There is a difference between being rich and wealthy. Rich is the measure of the value of one's personal possessions. Wealth is a state of mind that leads men to obtain riches or provisions along with power, prosperity, protection, and peace. You will know that you are wealthy when you have built something that has longevity and can be shared with more than one generation. If you are the only one benefiting from your money, you are rich not wealthy. One of the first steps required for every man to become wealthy is by becoming ego free. In order to be truly wealthy, a man must divorce himself from the person he pretends to be, disconnect his self from past achievements, and connect himself to the present so that his eyes can be open to see and his ears can open to hear. In that state of mind, a man will be able to receive the knowledge he needs through the Holy Spirit to create a future of wealth for 2 or 3 generations his family.

The average man who has no relationship with GOD or connection to the Spirit of GOD perceive wealth and riches as a type of omnipotence that serves their ego and allows them to pretend to be more than what they are by having more money and possessions than other men have. Men with a huge ego but no wealth or riches are the type of men who become preachers and politicians. These are professions where men who are nothing can be something. In these professions men can increase their wealth and riches by simply talking rather than creating or producing something. They trick you into believing that taking your money to build buildings is proof of their ability to create or produce. The only thing this proves is the wealth and riches they accumulate will always be at the expense of others.

Men who have a wealthy state of mind understand that they are only a conduit for money. They are a vehicle through which riches flow to be distributed to GOD's people. Since GOD does not muzzle the ox that treads the corn you can have as much of the riches you want as long as the overwhelming majority of it goes to GOD's people.

When men get greedy and become hoarders or excessive consumers GOD cuts off the flow to him and will begin to use someone else. Men who don't want to fall to the sin of greed must have a clear understanding that cash always flows through the righteous. There will always be more so there is no need to hoard.

Think about this for a minute. If you have $1 Billion you can eat and spend $10,000 every day and it will take you 273 years to consume it all. The reason people with $1 Million want more millions is they become lustful consumers. With $1 Million I can spend $2,740 per day for 1 year before consuming it all. To put this in context there are people who live on less than $2,800 per month. However, for the lustful consumer who never had a million before $2,800 is just a couple of hours at the strip club. And it's probably 2-3 times more if I am paying the bills for "my boys". As a result of being a hoarder, greedy, and lustful he will consume his entire $1 Million in less than 1 year.

Americans spend over $3 Billion every year on luxury goods to make it look like they have money while they are actually struggling. However, they spend very few dollars annually on information that will teach them how to become wealthy and end their struggling. When I analyzed the statistics I was amazed to find that the money Americans do spend on information to end their struggle is almost always spent on a scam or a get rich quick scheme. I know a couple that were up to their eyeballs in debt who put $30,000 on a credit card to pay for a seminar on flipping houses. The only thing they learned from that seminar is to not do that again. They learned nothing about all of the tribulations that go into flipping houses. They were not taught about the very expensive problems they could run into, how to recover from those problems, or how to mitigate those costs by reducing spending in other areas. The scammers gave them all the shine about how flipping houses would make them millionaires and just threw them out there. Muppet News Flash: when people come to sell something that is supposed to make you rich quickly that is a scam designed to make them rich quick not you!

"...Blessed is the man that fears the Lord, that delights greatly in HIS commandments. His seed [children] shall be mighty upon earth: the generation of the upright shall be blessed. Wealth and riches shall be in his house: and his righteousness endures for ever (Psalm 112:1-3)."

"Every man also to whom GOD has given riches and wealth, and has given him power to eat thereof and to take his portion, and to rejoice in his labor; this is the gift of GOD (Ecclesiastes 5:19)."

GOD fearing church going men must develop a new attitude about money, life, and religion if they want to be wealthy the way GOD intended. Church and religion teaches you to pray for money to heap it upon your lust so that you can be a consumer of houses, cars, clothes, and things. However, GOD wants you to be wealthy beyond measure so that you can have more than enough to get the things you want as well as to help meet the needs of others. There was nobody in the patriarchy or the family of GOD in the Bible that was not very wealthy. Every man or family leader within the lineage of Abraham, Isaac, and Jacob were wealthy. GOD said that a good man leaves an inheritance for his children's children or for 3 generations. Therefore, HE provided an inheritance to 3 generations of the children of Israel as an example of how we must make 3 generations of our children wealthy. However, that wealth must come through the word of GOD to prevent our children from falling into greed and lustful consumerism through the prosperity message or the false doctrines of religion. In order for you and I to be wealthy the way GOD wants we must cast aside the ritualistic practices of religion and simply learn to be as GOD is.

In the Sermon on the Mount, where Jesus delivered what Bible scholars call the "beatitudes", He was teaching us the attitudes that we must be in order to be as He is. Jesus was not teaching us what to do He was teaching us what to be. Religion focuses us on what to do in order to be in right standing with GOD. However, Jesus taught us what to be in order to be in right standing with the father. Jesus said for you to be perfect as your Father in heaven is perfect. But religion teaches there is no such thing as perfection. Religion teaches that it is impossible for you to be perfect and it is blasphemy for you to believe that you can be as GOD is.

When it comes to executing a mission GOD sent you on or fulfilling your created purpose GOD expects you to do the work. But when it comes to ritualistic activities that we engage in to be in right standing with HIM GOD expects you to be not do. GOD wants you to be fasted not do fasting, to be in communion or in common union with Christ Jesus not do communion, and to be baptized not do baptism. Doing worship rather than being worshipful is a work of the flesh that unwittingly invites evil spirits to enter in our church services, in our homes, and in our bodies. This allows the works of the flesh listed in Galatians 5:19-21 to manifest in our lives which are: adultery, fornication, uncleanness, lasciviousness, idolatry, witchcraft, hatred, variance, emulations, wrath, strife, seditions, heresies, envying, murders, drunkenness, reveling, and so on.

Once these perversions appear we struggle to figure out why. We are doing church, doing fasting, doing worship, doing prayer, and doing communion so we believe that we are in righteousness. But, fervently engaging in religious practices through ritualistic works of the flesh is causing perversion. Whenever we find something wicked it was once good that the devil twisted and made evil. Our job is to twist that wicked thing back around and return it to its good state. Rather than doing religious rituals let's turn them around to see what GOD originally intended them to be before the devil's disciples made them evil. Let's examine the church rituals we love to "do" so that we can see why doing them has become evil:

Fasting – the traditional ritual of fasting that we practice proves that preachers either don't read the word or they care more about following their religious doctrine and tradition rather than the word of GOD. Depriving yourself of food or afflicting your soul to suffer physically is not the type of fasting GOD expects to see. The fasting that preachers lead you to do today is a Babylonian religious tradition practiced by idolaters to gain favor and receive blessings from their idol gods. Preachers have either knowingly or unknowingly deceived people into believing their Babylonian fasting tradition is acceptable to the True and Living GOD. However, GOD has stated clearly that if you are saved yet practice idolatry you have cut yourself out of your kingdom inheritance.

"For this you know, that **no** whoremonger, nor unclean person, nor covetous man, who is an **idolater**, has **any inheritance** in the kingdom of Christ and of GOD. Let no man deceive you with vain words: for because of **these** things comes the wrath of GOD upon the children of disobedience. Be not you therefore partakers with them for you were sometimes darkness, but now are you light in the Lord: walk as children of light... proving what is acceptable unto the Lord. And have no fellowship with the unfruitful works of darkness, but rather reprove them (Ephesians 5:5-11)."

In Isaiah 58:4-11 GOD tells you exactly what fasting is and what is acceptable to HIM.

"Behold, you fast for strife and debate and to smite with the fist of wickedness. You shall **not** fast as you do this day, to make your voice to be heard on high. Is it such a fast that I have chosen; a day for a man to afflict his soul? Is it to bow down his head as a bulrush, and to spread sackcloth and ashes under him? Will you call this a fast and an acceptable day to the Lord?

Is not **this** the fast that I have chosen: to loose the bands of wickedness, to undo the heavy burdens, and to let the oppressed go free, and that you break every yoke [debt, captivity, bondage]? Is it not to deal your bread to the hungry, and that you bring the poor that are cast out to your house, when you see the naked, that you cover him; and that you hide **not** yourself from your own flesh (Isaiah 58:4-7)?"

The purpose of fasting is not to inflict your flesh or to be able to hear from GOD but rather to learn to deny yourself. The number one personal development goal a man must achieve before he gets married and have babies is to become selfless. If he is not selfless in a relationship with a wife and children he will not have the discipline to deny himself so that he can provide for and protect his family properly. A man who is selfish cannot be given responsibility for a family because he does not have response ability. Therefore, the type of fasting that GOD prescribed is designed to teach men to do for others what they would normally do for their self. Fasting prepares you to pursue and complete your GOD ordained purpose and thus makes it easy for you to deny yourself, take up your cross, and follow Jesus.

Men who learn to fast properly receive the rewards they were looking for automatically.

"Then shall your light break forth as the morning and your health shall spring forth speedily: and your righteousness shall go before thee; the glory of the Lord shall be your reward. Then shall you call, and the Lord shall answer; you shall cry, and HE shall say: Here I am. If you take away from the midst of you the yoke [debt, captivity, bondage], the putting forth of the finger, and speaking vanity; and if you draw out your soul to the hungry, and satisfy the afflicted soul; then shall your light rise in obscurity, and your darkness be as the noon day: and the Lord shall guide you continually, and satisfy your soul in drought, and make fat your bones: and you shall be like a watered garden, and like a spring of water, whose waters fail not (Isaiah 58:8-11)."

Worship – means to take the word of GOD and go somewhere with it to advance the gospel of Jesus, preach the kingdom of GOD, and defeat the devil and his disciples. Jesus was able to defeat the tempting devil in Matthew 4:1-11 because He was worship full. Being full of the word He took it into battle and defeated the tempter. King David spent most of his days tending sheep which gave him a lot of time to read the word, play his instrument, and write songs for GOD. When the time came to fight Goliath David was worship full. He took the word of GOD from Deuteronomy 28:25-26 into battle with him and used it to prophesy that giant's defeat. He took 5 smooth stones

A NEW ATTITUDE

from a brook and hurled one of them into Goliath's forehead like a bullet. The stone was smooth is because it had been washed in the water by the word. If we learn to be worship full rather than doing worshiping, we will be able to defeat all enemies.

Pray – means to converse with, receive instructions from, and be in communication with GOD continuously which is why Luke 18:1 says men must always pray and 1 Thessalonians 5:17 says to pray without ceasing; it is impossible to always pray or to pray without ceasing when you do prayer therefore GOD expects you to be prayer FULL not do prayer.

Baptism – baptized means to be submerged in the water of the word as a way of life not a symbolic act. Baptism to a Greek man has about as much religious significance as when he dunks a doughnut in his coffee. John practiced water baptism as an interim measure before the baptism of the Holy Spirit who would come with Jesus because John was a forerunner of Christ. The baptism of the Holy Spirit occurs when you are baptized in the water of the word of GOD and you have been baptized into Christ or have put on Christ like a protective garment. Proof that you are baptized in the Holy Spirit is revealed when you are a living image of the word wherein people of the world can see you giving the word of GOD life service not lip service.

Communion – is described in John 17 where Jesus prayed for us to be one with Him as He is one with the Father. Communion means

103

to be in common union with Christ Jesus. It is not a symbolic act of drinking His blood like a vampire. We are in common union with Jesus Christ when we know Him in the power of His resurrection and the fellowship of His suffering.

Prophesying – is akin to preaching which is to speak the will of GOD in an effort to lead the people of GOD into the will and the way of GOD. In order to prophesy you must be prophetic or sent to speak the rhema word of GOD or to speak HIS will.

Speaking in Tongues – is when you say something in one of the many KNOWN language of the world that is NOT your natural language, native tongue, or one that you learned to speak. The language is given voice through you by the Holy Spirit and someone around you will know what you said. It is NOT that sha-sha, ba-ba, hecomininahonda language of religion which is what the Apostle Paul called "the unknown tongue". The word "tongues is plural right? So why is it that when preachers speak that tongue where no one knows what they are saying they all have the same ba-ba, la-la, sha-sha sound? That sound is babble that comes from the spirit of Babylon. Therefore, Paul instructed us in 1 Corinthians 14:5 to prophesy rather than speak in an unknown tongue because no one is edified by it since nobody knows what you are saying.

CHAPTER 8

RELIGION: THE BONDAGE OF BABYLON

"You took up the tabernacle of Moloch, and the star of your god Remphan, figures which you made to worship them: and I will carry you away beyond Babylon (Acts 7:43)."

When we engage in religious practices for a long period of time wherein we are doing worship rather than being worship FULL we give place to the devil and room for the spirit of Babylon to enter into our lives. We unwittingly fall into worshiping other gods and get carried away into and have to suffer the consequences of religious captivity. Jesus said in John 10:10 "I came that you might have life and to have it more abundantly." So, why are so many church people dying suddenly in their 40's, 50's, and 60's? Why is it that you are hearing every preacher in every church prophesying: GOD is "about to" or "getting ready to" bless you when everyone in church and the community that surround it appears to be cursed financially? GOD is not a man that HE would lie. HE promised to provide long life, prosperity and peace. So, why is our lives being cut short? Why do we continue to struggle in poverty? Why is there no peace in our minds and bodies? Why do church people seem to suffer every social and medical malady disproportionately?

The reason we are experiencing an abundance of problems instead of an abundance of prosperity is because we have been led unwittingly to worship pagan gods not the True and Living GOD. We have not been able to access the benefits of HIS New Covenant abundance because we have been led into satanic captivity through Babylonian worship. We are being destroyed due to a lack of knowledge because we've allowed ourselves to become children of satan and he is an abusive parent.

"And upon her forehead was a name written, mystery, Babylon the great, the mother of harlots and abominations of the earth (Revelation 17:5)."

This verse is describing a church that is out of GOD's order and following the abominations of Babylonian tradition. The first sign that a church is out of the Most High GOD's order is there will always be strong women led by weak men. This is the sign of the spirit of Jezebel because it operates in both men and women. There are 5 levels of devil according to Ephesians 6:12: flesh and blood, principalities, powers, rulers of darkness, and spiritual wickedness. Jezebel is a principalities demon that seeks to take dominion and authority over any municipal organization such as a family, church, or city. Men are usually in authority over these municipalities. So women are used through the spirit of Jezebel to usurp the man's authority. Jezebel works for Babylon which is a powers demon.

When the spirit of Jezebel is present in men they become weak and laid back. When that spirit is present in women they become strong, aggressive, and you will see them operating in the man's authority. There is nothing wrong with a woman being strong or aggressive. Strong and aggressive is only problematic when the woman's intent is to usurp the man's authority, operate in his position, or substitute her will for his will.

"And Miriam the prophetess, the sister of Aaron, took a timbrel in her hand; and all the women went out after her with timbrels and with dances. And Miriam answered them: sing you to the Lord for HE has triumphed gloriously (Exodus 15:20-21)."

Aaron, the brother of Moses, was a weak man who was easily influenced by his sister Miriam. Notice in Exodus 15:20 Miriam was not referred to by GOD as the Moses' sister but rather the sister of Aaron. The greatest obstacle the children of Israel had in the wilderness was their inability to overcome Babylonian worship and tradition because the spirit of Jezebel was plaguing them. Miriam kept the influence of the spirit of Jezebel alive and active among the children of Israel through music or repeatedly singing the songs they sang in captivity. Music is an essential element of Babylonian worship.

Miriam led the people to worship in Babylonian tradition by singing, dancing, and playing the tambourine and other women followed her.

There is nothing wrong with making a joyful noise unto the Lord, or singing, or praising and blessing HIS name with thanksgiving. However, we cannot do any of them in the Babylonian tradition. Psalm 100:4 says to enter into HIS gates with thanksgiving and into HIS courts with praise; be thankful to HIM and bless HIS name. We just have to stop the so-called "worship services" that lead GOD's people to worship in the Babylonian tradition of singing, dancing, and playing instruments like the children of Israel worshipped the golden calf.

When Moses came off the mountain the people were playing music and dancing before the pagan god they had made. In Exodus 32:8 GOD said: they turned aside quickly out of the way which I commanded them, made a golden calf, and worshipped it. You see, after people in church finish the Babylonian activities that lead them to believe they are worshiping GOD they turn aside quickly and begin to worship and praise their preacher. He is their golden calf. He is their pagan god. Notice how the women in church glorify a preacher just like Miriam.

GOD could have made Moses Pharaoh of Egypt and led him to free HIS people. But if GOD did that the people would have made Moses their god instead of HIM. If GOD had freed HIS people but left them in Egypt they would have never gotten the Egypt out of them. They would have continued to worship in the Babylonian tradition of Egypt so GOD led them out of Egypt. African-Americans must understand that GOD led us out of Africa so we would not continue in their culture, their traditions, and worship their gods. Yet, what do we see operating in the African-American community? We have so-called "conscious" people working daily to lead us to back to Egypt; to conform to Babylonian culture and traditions and to worship their gods. The two most dangerous people to the African American community are uninformed preachers and the so-called "enlightened" Negro.

"And seeing the multitudes, He [Jesus] went up into a mountain: and when He was set, His disciples came unto Him: and He opened His mouth, and taught them (Matthew 5:1-2)."

"And it came to pass, that as the people pressed upon Him [Jesus] to hear the word of GOD, He stood by the lake of Gennesaret, and saw two ships standing by the lake… and He entered into one of the ships, which was Simon's, and prayed him that he would thrust out a little from the land. And He sat down and taught the people out of the ship (Luke 5:1-3)."

Whenever Jesus came before the people to teach it was never preceded by a worship service. There was no singing, praise dancing, or instruments of music playing although they had instruments and could indeed praise, dance, and sing. Jesus is preeminent or the first example for us in all things. That means whatever we have seen Him do we should do. On the other hand, whatever we have not seen Him do we should not do either. Was praise dancing being done before Jesus preached? He didn't have women dancing so where did this practice come from? It came out of Babylonian worship tradition that is also designed to seduce men and lead them to do things they would not normally do.

"...when Herod's birthday was kept, the daughter of Herodias danced before them, and pleased Herod. Whereupon he promised with an oath to give her whatsoever she would ask. And she, being before instructed of her mother, said: Give me here John Baptist's head in a charger. And the king was sorry: nevertheless for the oath's sake, and them which sat with him at meat, he commanded it to be given her (Matthew 14:6-8)."

The mother in this scene who was obviously operating in the spirit of Jezebel apparently knew that Herod would be seduced by the dance and would give the girl an offer so she conspired with her daughter to ask for John the Baptist to be beheaded. Earth Wind and Fire had a song called "Magnetic" wherein they sang: "The rhythm of a dangerous dance sucks you in twice as fast; sucks you in, you'll never last." Praise dancing is a type of hypnotism designed to overcome men's resistance to evil spirits, which works the same way on a man's mind as pornography to suck them in twice as fast. One of the reasons Babylonian tradition is practiced heavily during worship is because the church is in rebellion as a result of being under the control of Jezebel who works for Babylon. Again, the primary sign of a church in rebellion is weak sinful men in positions of leadership along with women being led by other women to engage in rebellious activities.

"And Miriam and Aaron spoke against Moses because of the Ethiopian woman whom he had married: for he had married an Ethiopian woman. And they said: has the Lord indeed spoken only by Moses? Has HE not spoken also by us? And the Lord heard it (Numbers 12:1-2)."

Here we see more evidence that Aaron was a weak man being led by Miriam as evidenced by her name being written first in this scene. We see them rising up against Moses and challenging his authority because he married a Black woman. They also moved in sedition to push Moses out of his position of authority on the basis of their bigotry. You see, when the spirit of Jezebel is operating in people they will always find a reason to dishonor or be disrespectful to whom GOD honors or respects. Jezebel's goal in this attack was to take Moses' authority. You see, through the influence of Jezebel Miriam had already usurped Aaron's authority as the High Priest by leading him to take actions she wanted. However, she was really after Moses' authority. She wanted the people to view her as being led by GOD too. She said: GOD doesn't just speak to Moses; HE speaks to us, me and Aaron too. GOD heard this and HE was not pleased.

"And the Lord came down in the pillar of the cloud, and stood in the door of the tabernacle, and called Aaron and Miriam: and they both came forth. And HE said: hear now my words: If there be a prophet among you, I the Lord will make myself known unto him in a vision, and will speak unto him in a dream. My servant Moses is not so, who is faithful in all mine house. With him will I speak mouth to mouth, even apparently, and not in dark speeches; and the similitude of the Lord shall he behold: wherefore then were you not afraid to speak against my servant Moses? And the anger of the Lord was kindled against them; and HE departed. And the cloud departed from off the tabernacle; and, behold, Miriam became leprous, white as snow...

And Moses cried unto the Lord, saying: heal her now, O GOD... and the Lord said to Moses: If her father had spit in her face, should she not be ashamed seven days? Let her be shut out from the camp seven days and after that let her be received in again (Numbers 12:5-10 & 13-14)."

GOD said, oh, OK, Miriam you want people to know that I speak to you too? So, HE did indeed speak to Miriam and Aaron by calling them out in front of all the people. GOD chastised her in front of all the people. Then HE afflicted Miriam with leprosy which is a type of cancer and casted her out of the camp for 7 days as punishment. Notice GOD didn't do anything to Aaron because HE recognized Aaron was weak but Miriam was being led by the spirit of Jezebel into sedition. Aaron and all the people needed to see that sedition had to be cast out and Miriam was clearly the one who continually led the people to continue in Babylonian worship traditions through Jezebel's influence.

"And when Joshua heard the noise of the people as they shouted, he said unto Moses, there is a noise of war in the camp. And he [Moses] said: it is not the voice of them that shout for mastery neither is it the voice of them that cry for being overcome: but the noise of them that sing do I hear. And it came to pass, as soon as he came near unto the camp, that he saw the calf, and the dancing (Exodus 32:17-19a)."

"And the Lord plagued the people because they made the calf which Aaron made (Exodus 32:35)."

"They eat up the sin of my people and they set their heart on their iniquity. And there shall be, like people, like priest: I will punish them for their ways and reward them their doings (Hosea 4:8-9)."

You see, the people fall prey to poverty, plagues, and every imaginable malady impacts their community negatively because preachers are leading them to worship pagan gods. Present day church goers, much like the children of Israel in the wilderness, are unwittingly led to participate in pagan worship traditions. Modern day Christians who purport to be holy proudly proclaim to pray using a heavenly language. They are unaware that the language they call heavenly is the same language that people who followed Nimrod were made to use because they were in rebellion to the Most High GOD. GOD twisted their tongues and caused them to babble. Babble was the language GOD cursed the people of Babylon with so they could not prosper in their rebellion. GOD said in Genesis 11:7 "Let us go down and confound their language that they may not understand each other's speech." The so-called "prayer language" that preachers lead you to do is a Babylonian language designed by satan to get revenge against GOD for confusing his people's language. He wants to prevent the people of GOD from effectively communicating with each other or with GOD.

"...Moses saw that the people were naked; for Aaron had made them naked unto their shame among their enemies (Exodus 32:25)."

Anytime the spirit of Babylon is present there will be some type of deviant sexual activity present also. Babylonians liked to worship naked. Evidence of the Babylonian tradition in operation in today's church is women are coming in to worship in tight pants, form fitting dresses, and some actually half naked. I was seated in the church balcony one day and witnessed this woman parade herself past the pulpit in a dress so tight I could see the ripples of her abdominal muscles from that distance. There were doors to the left and right of the pulpit that led back to the bathrooms and the fellowship hall. She waited until everyone had just settled down after worship and the preacher was about 2 minutes into his sermon to walk down the aisle and past the pulpit in a florescent yellow dress that fit her body like spray paint. I was a good distance away from her and I could see that she didn't have on any underwear.

"Do you not know that the saints shall judge the world? And if the world shall be judged by you, are you unworthy to judge the smallest matters? Know you not that we shall judge angels? How much more [then] things that pertain to this life (1 Corinthians 6:2-3)?"

Churches that operate in Babylonian tradition allow women to come to church dressed half naked or suggestive. Preachers who proclaim to know the Bible falsely lead people to believe they are not supposed to judge one another. They use the "come as you are" marketing mantra to draw people in church but never teach them that they cannot stay as they are. They use the same marketing gimmicks as night clubs to keep church goers entertained so they will keep coming back. They allow women "praise dance" to draw in more men. However, that is the same type of dancing Babylonian women did in honor of their supreme creator Oludamaré. Preachers that operate in Babylonian tradition use music as a signal to command or let the people know that it is time to worship. But that is no different than the Babylonian king. He commanded people to begin to worship the golden image he set up as god whenever they heard the music begin.

"To you it is commanded, O people, nations, and languages, that at what time you hear the sound of the cornet, flute, harp, sackbut, psaltery, dulcimer, and all kinds of music, you fall down and worship the golden image that Nebuchadnezzar the king has set up (Daniel 3:4-5)."

You see, the devil is very slick and subtle. GOD said my people are destroyed for a lack of knowledge. That is because the devil and his disciples will always attack and destroy your relationship with GOD using things you don't know about. You don't know that much of the church worship tradition comes from voodoo rituals that were mixed with Roman Catholicism to make you believe you are worshiping the Most High GOD while in reality you are worshiping the devil. The devil has tried many ways throughout history to steal GOD's praise; to lead GOD's people to worship him. Since GOD's people are ever learning but never coming into the knowledge of truth even their preachers have been subtly deceived.

"Beware lest any man spoil you through philosophy and vain deceit, after the tradition of men, after the rudiments of the world, and not after Christ (Colossians 2:8)."

Again, the devil is very slick and subtle. He will show you exactly what he is doing to you because he knows you have been mentally conditioned to keep your religious traditions so you won't do anything about it. Your religiosity keeps you bound in spiritual captivity practicing his Babylonian traditions. To show you how satan programs very subtly, most people were sucked in by the movie "The Black Panther" which broke box-office records world-wide. However, that movie revealed the power in Babylonian rituals that many Christian preachers engage in willingly because they believe that power is GOD's anointing.

Like many Babylonian religions the movie depicted references to receiving power through a type of communion and ancestor worship. The newly appointed king drank an herbal potion that gave him power, he got buried in a symbolic death ritual, went into a dream state, visited the ancestors for advice and guidance, and was then raised from the dead in a position of power. The spirit of Babylon will always present images and symbolism that mimic the death, burial, and resurrection of Jesus in its false deities or pagan gods. The arena where the king met with his counsel was called "The City of the Dead" named after the necropolis in Egypt where some people to this very day live and work among the dead to be near ancient ancestors. Through Babylonian tradition the Scribes and Pharisees of Jesus' day also used herbs to give them power to ward off evil.

"Woe unto you scribes and Pharisees; hypocrites! For you pay tithe of mint and anise and cumin, and have omitted the weightier matters of the law, judgment, mercy, and faith (Matthew 23:23)."

"But woe unto you Pharisees for you tithe mint and rue and all manner of herbs, and pass over judgment and the love of GOD (Luke 11:42)."

Anise was used by church leaders in Jesus' day because they were supposed to increase psychic abilities and ward off the "evil eye" by those practicing magic. Its seeds were drunk as a tea to induce spiritual trances. Mint was used in Babylonian rituals to worship their fire god.

117

Cumin was used like a rabbit's foot to bring about good luck or a happy life. Rue was used to thwart evil influences. It was also thought to bestow second sight like the all seeing eye. Rue was also called the "Herb of Grace" when it was mixed in the holy water used by Catholic priests to sprinkle on people before High Mass.

In addition to the power received from herbs, there were two types of necklaces in the Black Panther movie that produced the armor or "covering" for physical protection: panther claws (represented light magic) and cowrie shells (represented dark magic). You will miss the cowrie shells if you are not paying attention. Right after Killmonger defeats T'Challa a woman puts a necklace with cowrie shells around his neck. Cowrie shells are used in divination rituals of many African religions such as Santeria, Candomblé and Umbanda. You will find many so-called "conscious" African American men and women wearing cowrie shells as necklaces, bracelets, or head ornaments. Women from African nations wear them as they dance in honor of their gods in the same manner as praise dancing is done in church.

Many African nations worship a supreme creator called Oludamaré who is served by lesser gods called Orishas (that are disembodied spirits or human spirit travelers). Oduduwa is their Jesus like figure who was born of Akamara or their type of Mary. These religions originated with the Yoruba, Bantu, and Fon tribes of Africa. The practice of these religions migrated to North and South America with the Portuguese slave trade where it incorporated many Roman

Catholic religious traditions and is now finding a major influence in the Black church's liturgy.

My PhD is in Religious Studies. So I have studied many of the 140,000 religions that there are in the world most of which originated on the continent of Africa. Umbanda blends many African religions with Catholicism and spiritism which teaches people to let their bodies be used as mediums to contact the spirit world for power and guidance. Umbanda is the foundation of many African religions therefore there are many Umbandan denominations. This is similar to the 14,000 Christian based religions and their denominations. Just as all Christian based religions proclaim the Most High GOD is the Supreme Creator and the Holy Spirit is their guide all Umbanda based religions believe Olodumaré is the supreme creator and Orishas are their guiding spirits.

We are seeing the Black church being heavily influenced by African or Babylonian religious tradition that invokes evil spirits or pagan gods. Take the introduction of mimes in worship services now. Where did this practice come from and what does a mime have to do with worshiping the True and Living GOD? The truth is mimes are used to worship pagan gods. Mimes are representations of the faceless ghost. Faceless ghosts are unaware of their identity. Thus, they borrow the looks of living people to shape their otherwise featureless faces with the likeness of others. They differ from a doppelganger in that they simply borrow the looks of anyone they can get close to. People of GOD must understand that mimes are faceless ghosts or evil spirits searching for an identity who will steal your identity if you allow them to.

CHAPTER 9

WALK NOT WITH THE UNGODLY

"Blessed is the man that walk not in the counsel of the ungodly, nor stand in the way of sinners, nor sit in the seat of the scornful (Psalms 1:1)."

"In transgressing and lying against the Lord, and departing away from our GOD, speaking oppression and revolt, conceiving and uttering from the heart words of falsehood... judgment is turned away backward and justice stands afar off: for truth is fallen in the street, and equity cannot enter (Isaiah 59:13-14)."

The average Christian today cannot find the way to the truth and the light that leads to abundant life because we have been conditioned to walk in the counsel of the ungodly. The majority of today's preachers, pastors, ministers, and elders are unable to lead you to the truth because they have been led unwittingly to walk in the counsel of the ungodly their selves. They have been led to believe that homiletics, which is a curious art or a type of voodoo, is the art of preaching. They have no clue that homiletics is actually an art of spell casting and mesmerizing that is a form of witchcraft. Homiletics is designed to influence your mind to make you open your spirit so they can breathe whatever spirit they have in them into you.

Preachers have also been led to believe that Hermeneutics is the science of interpreting the Bible. If you know that GOD designed the Bible to be understood not interpreted you will immediately know there has to be something that GOD did not intend going on in the practice of Hermeneutics. That is because Hermeneutics is also a curious art or form of witchcraft that was introduced into Christianity. Credit for its origin is given to a Greek or Egyptian god (depending on who you believe stole what history from who) named Hermes Trismegistus. He is also credited with tens of thousands of high level works of literature used to train all the Egyptian priests. Hermetic literature is said to contain ancient knowledge of spells and induction procedures on the art of imprisoning the souls of demons or angels known as the Hermetic Seal. But now the Hermetic Seal, this demonic spell, is being used in church on GOD's people to capture their souls.

The Hermetic Seal is applied to your mind through homiletics which is designed to make your mind impervious to outside influence. It is a spell designed to hold you in mental and spiritual captivity once it captures your soul because your soul is the mind of your spirit. The Hermetic Seal binds your mind and makes you stay in bondage even when you know you are being held against your will. The thing about the power of hermeneutics and homiletics is it works once you apply the science whether you know what you are doing or not. To give them the benefit of the doubt I would say the average preacher has no clue he is using curious arts or witchcraft to keep people coming to his church. He just knows that there's something about his preaching that makes them stay even when he gets caught in any number of sinful misdeeds.

I strongly caution you preachers to stop using the science of homiletic and hermeneutics or witchcraft to grow your church and/or retain your members. Jesus said if I be lifted up I will draw all men unto me. The only thing you have to do is lift up the name of Jesus if you want your church to grow. If you teach in a way that causes your people to grow, they will bring other people, and your membership will grow. You don't need Hermeneutical witchcraft to interpret the Bible because GOD intended for the Bible to be understood not interpreted.

The Bible interprets and confirms itself because it is built on the two or three witness principle. Jesus said: out of the mouth of 2 or 3 witnesses let every word be established. The truth of word of GOD therefore is established on the 2 or 3 witness principle so this is why we have 4 gospels. Each gospel has 3 other gospels that serve as witnesses to confirm and interpret them. Therefore, if you are a preacher and you want your church to prosper financially and have the population grow, you simply need to preach the TRUTH of the gospel.

Babylonian Worship Leads to Poverty and Death

The children of Israel operated in a vicious cycle where they would have peace and prosperity with GOD for many years but then they would turn away and begin to fornicate with other gods. Each time they chose to worship other gods they were always led away by the spirit of Babylon influencing their leaders. Luke 4:13 says when the devil had finished temping or trying to entice Jesus to worship him, he departed from him for a season. You see, when the devil come to tempt you to turn away from GOD and you resist him, as James 4:7 says, he will flee but it will only be for a season. The devil will always come back and approach you at a different angle but it will always be that same Babylonian spirit that he sends to capture you. Take notice of 2 Chronicles 15:3 which helps us to see that when the spirit of Babylon comes it will always be after a season when the children of Israel has not been worshiping the True and Living GOD for a long time because they had no teaching priest who taught the truth of the word of GOD.

"And in those times there was no peace to him that went out, nor to him that came in, but great vexations were upon all the inhabitants of the countries. And nation was destroyed of nation, and city of city: for God did vex them with all adversity (2 Chronicles 15:5-6)."

We see the world in same condition today because for a long time now people have been going to church and proclaiming to worship god but they have not been worshiping the True and Living GOD. As a result of the prosperity message plaguing the church for nearly 40 years the people have not had a person who occupies the 5 fold ministry office of the teacher to teach them the truth of the word of GOD. This vacuum has given room for the spirit of Babylon to creep in. The devil sent this spirit in preaching prosperity but enticing GOD's people through the sins of lust and greed promising they would receive much for little. The Most High GOD does indeed want HIS people to prosper but not to pursue prosperity through lust and greed. Thus, for almost 40 years the people of GOD have gone whoring after the idol gods of wealth and they have been vexed with all kinds of adversity as a consequence.

"And in the thirty and eighth year of Asa king of Judah began Ahab the son of Omri to reign over Israel: and Ahab the son of Omri reigned over Israel in Samaria twenty and two years. And Ahab the son of Omri did evil in the sight of the Lord above all that were before him. And it came to pass, as if it had been a light thing for him to walk in the sins of Jeroboam the son of Nebat, that he took to wife Jezebel the daughter of Ethbaal king of the Zidonians, and went and served Baal, and worshipped him (1 Kings 16:29-31)."

Ahab and Jezebel were king and queen over Israel who had hundreds of false prophets that introduced Baal worship among GOD's people and brought in sexual sin as well as child sacrifice. Whenever the people of GOD are in a prolonged state of spiritual fornication and sin GOD always sends a man to warn them to repent before HE rains judgment down upon them. Preachers need to quickly come to the understanding that judgment begins as the household of faith. That means GOD's judgment always falls on preachers first.

"And it came to pass, when Ahab saw Elijah that Ahab said unto him: Are you he that troubles Israel? And he answered, I have not troubled Israel; but you, and your father's house, in that you have forsaken the commandments of the Lord, and you have followed Baalim. Now therefore send, and gather to me all Israel unto Mount Carmel, and the prophets of Baal four hundred and fifty, and the prophets of the groves four hundred, which eat at Jezebel's table... and Elijah came unto all the people and said: How long halt you between two opinions? If the Lord be GOD, follow him: but if Baal, then follow him. And the people answered him not a word (1 Kings 18:17-21)."

"Then the fire of the Lord fell... and when all the people saw it they fell on their faces: and they said: The Lord, HE is the GOD; the Lord, he is the GOD. And Elijah said unto them: Take the prophets of Baal; let not one of them escape. And they took them: and Elijah brought them down to the brook Kishon and slew them there (1 Kings 18:38-40)."

The religious leaders of Jesus' day could not see who He was because they were looking at Him the wrong way. Their minds became impervious to His truth due to the false teachings and the false prophecy of their religious doctrine and traditions. Their other problem was the greed of their religiosity. They weren't so much excited about the coming of the Messiah as they were about the benefits they would get as a result of His Kingdom being established on earth. They were looking for the leader of an army (The Lord of Hosts) that would overthrow the Roman Government, end its oppressive rule, and establish the religious reign of the Kingdom of Heaven on earth. False religious doctrine taught them HOW this was going to be done but it was wrong. Since they didn't see Jesus doing what they believed the Messiah was supposed to do they were offended. Even John the Baptist began to question whether or not Jesus was indeed the Messiah. He sent his disciples to ask Jesus: "Are you the one or shall we look for another?"

You see, religion and religious doctrine prevented even the very elect of GOD's people from seeing the truth. When the reality did not agree with their false prophecy they decided Jesus was the problem. Their minds could not make the adjustment from what they believed to receive the truth. They never stopped to ask their selves: could we have misinterpreted the prophecy? They couldn't do it because they were sold out to their doctrine. The same thing is occurring today. The people of GOD refuse to question the doctrine and traditions of their denominations. Consequently, false doctrine and religious teaching is preventing them from seeing the truth and being free. So, they remain in poverty without the power and provision contained in the kingdom of GOD.

"In transgressing and lying against the Lord, and departing away from our GOD, speaking oppression and revolt, conceiving and uttering from the heart words of falsehood… judgment is turned away backward and justice stands afar off: for truth is fallen in the street, and equity cannot enter (Isaiah 59:13-14)."

GOD's people are becoming more and more frustrated and angry wondering why they are not receiving their breakthrough. They continue to pray and beg GOD to give them what HE has already placed inside of them or within their reach. The way most of us have been taught in church is backward or opposite to the way of the word of GOD. Our heads have been turned away from the truth of the word. When the answer to our prayer does fall through the windows of heaven we can't see it because we are facing the wrong way. Ergo, we leave our blessing lying on the ground and the devil sends his kids to pick it up.

"…the wealth of the sinner *is* [was] laid up for the just (Proverbs 13:22)."

"…the children of this world are in their generation wiser than the children of light (Luke 16:8)."

The sinner is able to claim the wealth that <u>was</u> laid up for the just because the minds of the children of light have been darkened with the deception of religion. We can accept that the only way GOD does HIS work in the earth is through man. We believe that GOD's system of delivering financial and spiritual assistance to HIS people is through other people. The problem comes when religion adds the false doctrine that blessings come through the Old Testament system of mercy rather than the New Testament dispensation of grace. Religion teaches that through the system of mercy, the blessings you receive (which you don't really deserve or that are an unmerited favor) are dispensed from an external source.

The truth is those blessings are drawn to you from other people through an internal source or the power of GOD working in you. The Apostle Paul said in Ephesians 3:20: GOD can give you things that are exceedingly above what you could even think to ask for but it is according to the power that is working in you. Jesus said in John 15:7 that if you live in me and my word lives in you, you can ask for whatever you want and it will be done for you. 1 Corinthians 3:16 says that you are the temple of GOD and the Spirit of GOD lives in you! Therefore, in the system of grace blessings are accessed internally. Luke 17:21 says: the Kingdom of GOD is within you. The Kingdom of GOD is the New Testament system dispensation of grace. The children of GOD don't have to beg, "Lord have mercy", because we have access to HIS grace.

"...take no thought, saying, what shall we eat or what shall we drink or wherewithal shall we be clothed ...for your heavenly Father knows that you have need of all these things. But you seek first the kingdom of GOD and HIS righteousness; and all these **things** shall be added unto you (Matthew 6:31-33)."

Grace is the power of GOD that works in people who are living in HIS covenant. Money is a form of grace or power that is dispensed to us through the kingdom of GOD. GOD gives you money for two reasons: to meet your needs and to fulfill your purpose. You need money to draw the cash required to cover your normal living expenses. This is why Jesus said that GOD knows you have need of these things. This is also why GOD said in Deuteronomy 8:18 that HE has given you power to get wealth. The only two stipulations GOD placed on your acquisition of wealth is that you be in right standing with HIM and you must seek to obtain it through the power of HIS economic supply system. Money, which is the spiritual energy or idea that leads to wealth, comes through the Kingdom of GOD system of wealth distribution.

The system of the Kingdom of GOD works on principles. GOD made those principles universal so that everyone could have an equal opportunity to apply them uniformly and become wealthy. Those principles will work for whoever works them and they work better for those who understand how to work them best. The reason some people are wealthy while others are rich and some are poor is due to their understanding of the system. Quarterbacks who understand their team's system play better in the game. The more people understand the system of the Kingdom of GOD's principles and the level of power those principles generate the greater level of wealth the system will create for them. Those with a higher level of understanding can generate a greater level of power therefore they produce more wealth.

If we work to receive money to fulfill our GOD ordained purpose through the Kingdom of GOD, all the money that we require is supplied. Since money comes in the form of spirit energy the devil tries to use spiritual deception through false religious doctrine to keep us from receiving it. The enemy simply hides the truth about what money really is and confuses us into believing that money and cash is the same thing and that they are both evil things The adversary does this to trick us into rejecting true power and wealth and thereby inhibit the plan of GOD to make the entire earth like the Garden of Eden; a place of wealth and peace.

Buying into the deception that money or cash is evil has caused many of GOD's people to fall into a cycle of poverty for many generations because without truth the lie is difficult to overcome. Poverty generates crime which destroys the peace of an environment. Money is spiritual energy that must have an environment of agreement or peace in order to be productive and generate wealth. Thus, in order to receive money through the kingdom of GOD you must be in covenant, in oneness, and at peace with the True and Living GOD.

The First 48

"Study to show yourself approved to GOD a workman that need not to be ashamed, rightly dividing the word of truth (2 Timothy 2:15)."

Studying the word of GOD shortly after receiving it works on the same principle of that police based reality TV show called "The First 48" where they investigate real life murder cases. In a homicide investigation, if you don't solve that crime within the first 48 hours, the probability of solving it drops dramatically. This is why Jesus said in Luke 6:47-49:

"Whosoever comes to me, and hear my sayings and do them, I will show you to whom he is like: he is like a man which built a house, and dug deep, and laid the foundation on a rock: and when the flood arose, the stream beat vehemently upon that house, and could not shake it: for it was founded upon a rock. But he that hears and does nothing is like a man that without a foundation built a house upon the earth; against which the stream did beat vehemently, and immediately it fell; and the ruin of that house was great."

If you don't study a book like this to get understanding or do something with what you learned within the first 48 hours of receiving it, the probability of you getting **any** value out of the teaching to benefit your family drops dramatically. The devil will cause issues to come up like storms in your life to steal the value. Then, you will never understand the mysteries which were revealed to empower you. When you get a teaching like this you must listen to it at least 3 or 4 times in its entirety and you must make notes on how you are going to use the knowledge to improve your life and the lives of your family financially. Alright? Amen!

Giving all praise, honor, and glory to GOD… in Jesus' name!

ABOUT THE AUTHOR

For over 30 years Dr Will has helped men repair their personal and professional relationships. He holds a PhD in Biblical Studies and authored many books: including Strengthening the Family, Relationships 911, How to Avoid Bad Relationships, Healing the Wounded Woman, Money DOES Grow on trees, Secrets of the Fortune 500, and more. Dr Will used the power of excellence in relationships to lead thousands of men to become successful by helping them create a better version of themselves. He used this skill to produce highly proficient employees, championship sports teams, and influence drug dealers to turn their illegal operations into legitimate businesses. Dr Will also conducts award winning seminars for men in the areas of domestic violence prevention and awareness, personal development, and family enrichment, along with wealth building and management. Visit www.drwillspeaking.com for more information.

www.ingramcontent.com/pod-product-compliance
Lightning Source LLC
Chambersburg PA
CBHW021338090426
42742CB00008B/653